Gateway to an Enlightened World

Collective Life Lessons to Support Planetary Transformation

Gateway to an *Enlightened World*

Collective Life Lessons to Support Planetary Transformation

Compiled by Dr. Ruth Anderson

Gateway to an Enlightened World: Collective Life Lessons to support Planetary Transformation
Published by SageHouse Press
Louisville, CO

Copyright ©2020 Ruth Anderson. All rights reserved.

No part of this book may be reproduced in any form or by any mechanical means, including information storage and retrieval systems without permission in writing from the publisher/author, except by a reviewer who may quote passages in a review.

All images, logos, quotes, and trademarks included in this book are subject to use according to trademark and copyright laws of the United States of America.

Publisher's Cataloging-in-Publication data
Names: Anderson, Ruth Elaine, 1960-.
Title: Gateway to an enlightened world: collective life lessons to support planetary transformation. / Dr. Ruth Anderson.
Description: First trade paperback original edition. | Louisville [Colorado] : SageHouse Press, 2020. | Also available as an ebook.
Identifiers: ISBN 978-0-9984573-6-9
Subjects: LCSH: Spiritualism. | Archangels. | Spirituality—New Age movement.
BISAC: BODY, MIND, SPIRIT / Inspiration & Personal Growth | BODY, MIND & SPIRIT / Angels & Spirit Guides.
Classification: LCC BF1277.A1 | DDC 133—dc22

Cover Design: Sue Broome
Editor: Dido Clark
Layout: Karen Tants

QUANTITY PURCHASES: Schools, companies, professional groups, clubs, and other organizations may qualify for special terms when ordering quantities of this title. For information, email SageHousePress@gmail.com

Book is printed in the United States of America.

All rights reserved by Ruth Anderson and SageHouse Press.

DEDICATION

This book is lovingly dedicated to Archangel Michael, the brilliant mastermind who called each author to come to the table and be transformed as a result of doing so.

This book is also dedicated to the authors, with such gratitude that you were open to experiencing life-changing spiritual transformation and were willing to share your story with others. I have such love for each and every one of you and can't wait to see where your journeys take you. Thank you each for following your calling and for walking with me in mine. I know that the world is a better place simply because you all are in it!

Gateway to an Enlightened World: Collective Life Lessons to Support Planetary Transformation

Proudly Sponsored by

Linda Patten
Be Courageous, Dare to become a Comfluential™ Leader
Leadership Expert, Trainer for Women Entrepreneurs and Changemakers. Founder & CEO of Dare2Lead/Creator Awaken the Leader. Creator of The Art of Herding Cats: Leading Teams of Leaders. Creator of Seeds of a Movement for Change

Dare 2 Lead
WITH Linda
www.dare2leadwithlinda.com

RHG Media Productions
Rebecca Hall Gruyter is the founder/Owner of Your Purpose Driven Practice, Creator of the Women's Empowerment Conference events and TV show, Creator of the Speaker Talent Search, and International Best-Selling Author. She is also the Producer and Creator of "Empowering Women, Transforming Lives," a popular radio show released on multiple channels and networks around the world.
www.yourpurposedrivenpractice.com

AT THE ROUND TABLE

I am repeatedly shown a vision of a round table in a space in the ethereal realm. The players seated around it vary, but Archangel Michael, Archangel Raphael, Divine Mother, and I are constants. It is what some might call a "war room," although it is certainly not war that is being discussed. It is divine love, and how to expand awareness of divine love in the earthly realm. Together we strategize how to bring Heaven to Earth.

Enlightened World, a safe space for bringing together a conscious community, was one of the ideas birthed at the Round Table; as was hosting a Summit called Enlightened Women ~ Enlightened You, including who to interview and what questions to ask. It was at the Round Table that Archangel Michael shared the idea of compiling the Gateway to an Enlightened World anthologies. They would provide a platform for the summit speakers and participants to share their stories of personal spiritual transformation. The hope was that others who read these stories would have their hearts touched and their awareness expanded.

God, or Source, reminds me that the Round Table and all that attend there are extensions of divine love. We are not separate from God, but all are one with Source and each other. So, really, the vision of bringing Heaven to Earth is already done, as divine love is within us and always has been. So, perhaps, the message to share is: Welcome Home to the understanding that you always had. Welcome Home to Enlightened World.

Dr. Ruth Anderson
Founder of Enlightened World
Summit Host, Award Winning Author, Spiritual Counselor
www.enlightenedworld.online

CONTENTS

Dedication..5

Proudly Sponsored by...................................7

At the Round Table......................................8

Chapter 1: The Many Facets of "Letting Go"
    By Anayah Joi Holilly............................13

Chapter 2: Mother Teresa-Your Mission is Calling You
    Channelled by Neelam Minocha..................21

Chapter 3: Who or What is God?
    By Debbie N. Goldberg...........................29

Chapter 4: The Question I am Asked So Often
    By Ivana Vozzo Morano..........................39

Chapter 5: Divine Mother and the Pearl
    By Stephen Altair................................49

Chapter 6: Calling on Angels
    By Olivia Parr-Rud..............................61

Chapter 7: River Guide
    By Elisabeth Williams...........................71

Chapter 8: The Road More Frequently Traveled
  By Nancy Tarr Hart, PhD..............................75

Chapter 9: Love Yourself and Your Dog Will Follow
  By Kristy Bright..85

Chapter 10: Through the Fire and Out the Other Side—The Phoenix Has Risen
  By Teri Angel..93

Chapter 11: "Come Dance with Me" Step onto Your Spiritual Path
  By Linda Dierks..101

Chapter 12: Reach Beyond the Stars
  By Sue Broome...109

Chapter 13: Awakening to An Empowered Life
  By Stacie Harder.......................................115

Chapter 14: Contemplations on Oneness and Resistance
  By Mira Rubin..125

Chapter 15: My Mantra
  By Christine Crockett Smith.....................131

Chapter 16: What I have created, I have the power to change!
    By Debbie Garcia………………………………….137

Chapter 17: Surrendering to Spirit
    By Keleena Malnar and Yeshayah……………….141

Chapter 18: Steps of Healing from Abuse
    By Monica Augustine……………………………..153

Chapter 19: Readings From our Enlightened Angels
    By Sheryl Glick…………………………………….163

Chapter 20: Grandma's Infinite Healing Blessings
    By Sommer Joy Ramer……………………………177

Chapter 21: The Enlightened Women ~ Enlightened You Summit Unpacked
    Contributed by Dr. Ruth Anderson……………..183

1

The Many Facets of "Letting Go"

By Anayah Joi Holilly

I am a lightworker, a volunteer here on this planet. I am also an empath. I'm learning to recognize and let go of what is not mine to experience.

My beautiful, happy, peaceful life felt shattered the day my dad made his crossing in 2017. How could my dad die— my beautiful dad, the man I trusted and felt safe with? I was 60, yet I felt as though I were a little girl of 5, suddenly without her dad to look after her, to make sure she was safe. On that day, my blood pressure skyrocketed to astronomical heights. It's the little things sometimes that make all the difference: doors opening or closing, corners turned, choices made. My sister asked me if I'd like a cup of coffee. I desperately wanted to say yes, but something made me say no. With a blood pressure reading of 209, imagine if I'd said yes, and added caffeine into my system. I can see how protected I was in that moment.

A new journey of letting go had begun; I just didn't know it at that time. Nine weeks later, my mum made her transition.

Though they'd been divorced over 30 years, and my mum and beautiful stepmother became close friends, dad was still my mum's rock. When he died, she just couldn't go on, and she told me she was tired, she'd had enough. I thought I could be enough, enough reason for her to stay. I thought I could help her through that time, it would all be OK, surely? I'm the oldest child, so it's my job to make sure the family stays together, right? I'd always felt that way, I had taken on that role, unbeknownst to myself, or my parents, when I was five and carried it in my subconscious.

Mum went into the hospital with a clot in her lung. She'd been through this before and was absolutely fine. I spoke to her on the phone. We laughed, we joked about her eating all the ice cream, and where was mine? We had a wonderful time together, our last.

The hospital was a couple of hours away, and my eldest daughter, who wasn't working that day, offered to take me to see mum, as I'm not able to drive that distance myself. I didn't feel compelled to go to her. I still can't believe it. "Why don't we leave it until Sunday when we can take the kids? Mum will be feeling so much better by then, and you know how much mum loves seeing them." It took me a long time to come to terms with that, and in writing this, sobbing, I realize I still am. That was a Tuesday evening. I spoke to mum the next morning; she sounded very tired. She was dead by that afternoon. I was at the hairdresser's and my sister called and said she thought that mum had just had a stroke. She was speaking to her on the phone and mum lost her words. Terrified, I called the hospital. The doctor confirmed mum had had a stroke. I learned later that the medication administered to dissolve the clot caused a series of catastrophic strokes. Sitting in the hairdresser's chair, I spoke to my unconscious, precious mum. A nurse held the phone to her ear. I poured my love into my words. "Mummy, I love you. The angels are waiting to receive you. It's OK for you to let go whenever you are ready. Thank you for being my mum. I will love you forever."

I could feel her there, I could feel our connection, I could feel the sacredness of the moment even as I sat in the hairdresser's chair, with other clients around me, gently supported by the wonderful woman who was owner of the salon and my hairdresser who gently said, "We all understand. You take your time, spend this time with your mum."

What a pure blessing. I was on the phone for about 15 minutes I guess; I didn't want to hang up, I didn't want to say goodbye. Eventually, I felt the earthly threads between us getting thinner and thinner, and I knew I had to hang up the phone, to give mum permission to let go. The terrible pain. I was about to become an orphan.

My life with my parents was never perfect. It was full of ups and downs, cross words, misunderstandings, coming to terms with each other, beautiful hugs, love, support, periods of time where we didn't speak, and treasured moments. We learned how to communicate in ways I'd always dreamed of over their last few years; so precious. That is something I don't have to let go, it will remain with me forever. Choosing to let go of recrimination, to embrace gratitude for all I did appreciate about my mum especially

(I'd already found that pathway with my dad) opened many doors for me.

I felt bruised, battered, shattered into a million pieces. The landscape of my life had been torn apart: how do I go on without my mum and my dad? My inner child felt lost and alone. I gathered my children and loved ones close; we loved and cherished, supported, and nurtured each other. As we'd done for dad, we gave mum a beautiful memorial service, a celebration of her life. That was very healing, but it was also the end of all the busy-ness, all the activity. The day-to-day nothingness began. My blood pressure was still raging. There were so many times I truly believed my body couldn't sustain life under those conditions; even medicated, it was still so high on a day-to-day basis.

The thing that scared me the most wasn't that I would die, it was that I would die and my children would have to suffer what I was suffering. That fear seemed unbearable, unendurable to me. That was January 2017. By March, a treasured relationship began to fall apart at the seams, and within a matter of weeks, I realized I would have to let it go, to release it to the Light. I fell to my knees. I crashed. I felt devastated by the choices I knew were the right ones for me to live with integrity.

I cried to God, "How do I let go! I don't want to let go. I have to fix this. Help me!" This was a time of great internal conflict for me. My old patterns of people-pleasing, rescuing, and co-dependency were raging within my mind. Yet my inner voice, my inner truth, spoke to me of the old beliefs I was laying to rest, of our souls' contracts, of the truth that only love is real, of my free-will opportunities to step outside the victim roles I'd been unconsciously setting up and playing, and into the freedom of my authentic self.

The internal struggle was exhausting, yet I didn't know how to let go, how to break out of this destructive cycle. Something that really bothered me incredibly deeply was this: I am a spiritual woman, I know my parents are safe, happy, and well. They've visited me, reassured me time and time again. I know the love of my released relationship is alive and well, soul-to-soul, even as it seems to disintegrate on a human level. I knew everything was in divine order, that it was part of my soul contract we'd all agreed to before we incarnated into this life experience together. So why, why in God's name can I not be OK with it all? Why can't I seem to let go and move past it into peace and acceptance?

This fear, this longing for what feels lost, for what I cannot "fix" was like a living hell. Yet, at the same time, I was living my truth, my integrity. It took a lot of to-ing and fro-ing, ups and downs, of imagined conversations, as if I could get the other person to see what I so desperately wanted them to see. In other words, I was still caught up in that struggle of, "I can fix this, I can make this all come right!" in the ways that I wanted it to. The great journey of letting go, the scaling of sheer cliffs of terror, the descent into acceptance and peace, was not an easy one for me and I'm still finding my way. But, I am conscious that this opportunity is mine for the choosing, to remember I am a holy child of God, that only love is real, that my soul contracts are sacred, and not a punishment, and they are magnificent opportunities to free myself of the illusion fear, of shame, failure, and recriminations.

There are days I feel completely at peace with it all. Other days I feel the internal struggle and those distracting conversations run through my mind. I'm becoming much more aware of those conversations and how destructive they really are. It's better, easier—mostly. It took me quite a while to remember to use the following prayer, but once I did, and started to appreciate it and pray it again slowly, piece by piece, I began to feel more balanced, more in alignment. "I am willing to release that part of me which angers (or saddens, or is infuriating, etc.) me, when I think of you."

Knowing something is valuable, and experiencing it in service to one's self, are two very different things. It was not enough for me to know it in my head, I needed to choose to remember to bathe in its calm waters. I am very blessed. I am choosing to free myself from the illusion that I am somehow a victim and move into the truth that I am victorious, divinely loved, a divine creation, and that being here on earth at this time is a privilege. Over the past few days, after a period of blood pressure calm, my blood pressure skyrocketed again. Why? Why? Why? What is it trying to tell me and why can't I get it?! Why can't I stop it from happening?!

Just yesterday, while speaking with a dear friend who has a lot of spiritual wisdom and who so generously shares it with me, I had a major emotional release mid-conversation. In a flash of insight, I suddenly understood that I've been punishing myself as though I deserve to have a stroke myself for not saving my parents from having theirs. My heart felt like it was breaking with the pain of their deaths all over again, of what they might have felt, yet at the same time, it was so cathartic, so freeing to finally, finally, understand what my blood pressure has been telling me all this time: I am not responsible for my parents' strokes. It is not my journey to live their lives, or their deaths. It is not my responsibility to take any of this on as my own or as some kind of misplaced penance. I need to let it all go.

I don't know what that's going to look like for me yet, but I do know that having this insight is the next part of this journey. It's the first page of the next chapter. Letting go of everything that doesn't serve me sounds so easy, doesn't it? The reality is that it's a step-by-step process, sometimes with clarity, sometimes it's the opposite. Sometimes the steps feel like leaps, and other times they feel minuscule. My friend reminded me that the threads of our life experiences are sometimes lifetimes in the making. By healing mine in the here and now for myself, a ripple effect is created. I am so incredibly blessed in my life. I have wonderful relationships that are strong, respectful, nurturing, supportive, and loving, including, and most importantly, the relationship I have with myself.

With love, Anayah Joi Holilly
September 2019

About Anayah Joi Holilly

A self-love advocate, Anayah Joi Holilly is a woman who has walked many paths throughout her life, including those of overwhelming sadness, pain, and sorrow.

These paths have helped reveal to her the bedrock of joy, peace, inspiration, divine love, and her own divine personal connection, all which were already within her, and how to live with and through it all to embrace (more and more) her own divine nature, which she believes to be the core of every human being.

Anayah is the creator of Angel Light 777, a non-denominational gathering place where she shares the angels' love, resources, support, and wisdom, and is the founder, radio host, and executive producer of Angel Heart Radio. She is also a certified Angel Intuitive with advanced training, self-love advocate, and soon to be published contributing author in the 1000 Ripple Effects project. Her upcoming book is with the angels, *THE ANGEL CODE – Journey Into The Words Whispered to Me.*

Anayah is passionate about helping others feel their own ever-present connection with the angels, in ways that are meaningful to them.

Website: Angel Light777
Facebook: @AngelHeartRadio

2

Mother Teresa – Your Mission is Calling You

Channelled by Neelam Minocha

Peace dear ones, create peace in a world of chaos…
Eliminate the chaos in your lives by quietening the mind.
Go to the core of your being and breathe in life…
Breathe in gratitude…
Breathe in light…
As humans you have forgotten just what you can be grateful for.

I saw the suffering in the world, impoverished children crying by the roadside for love, for food, for human touch, what didn't my eyes witness… the suffering of mankind, of children hungry for love.

Human compassion dear ones, human compassion and love for your fellow humans… eliminating suffering all around. But first start with the self.

What within you is not at peace?

Where do you need more compassion for self?

What are you doing for others that you are not doing for yourself?

Are you living, giving, and being kind to yourself? Because only then can you give to others from a space of unconditional love.

What are you seeking outside that cannot be found by going within? Go into the depths of your soul and heal. You are needed as peaceful warriors to transcend the suffering and bring peace in your world.

Each one of you so powerful… simple acts of kindness that ripple out and inspire others on their path. Don't give up… keep going, keep opening your hearts and be kind, above all be kind with your words as your words can be like daggers in the soul—the scars stay for a very long time.

Why hurt yourselves in the first place, be kind dear ones, be gentle, be grateful and start your day with peace in your soul so that your day ebbs and flows.

Let go of rigid views and fixed ideas and being stuck in beliefs.

Flow like water and move with the tides of change. Be willing to change direction where your heart takes you.

The more you surrender, the more you will experience the flow of love and life.

We are with you through this transition. You have so much love and compassion to give but you must release the victim mentality that keeps you suffering and in pain.

There is always someone worse off... what can we do collectively to make the world a better place? Look around you... start with your home, then your area, then spread out to the world.

It starts with you taking action. Be love and compassion in action creating ripples of change.

Be fearless, be willing and we will send you help and support.

Take the steps forward and watch the magic unfold. We are with you dear ones. We are with you.

Peace begins within our soul and then we spread peace to all around us by being that vibration in ourselves. The world has lost its way, it is too attached to external commodities and ignores what is taking place within. Greed for things outweighs the need for food. This is the dis-ease of the 21st century—attachment to things...

Simplify your lives dear ones, simplify if you want peace.

Find what ignites your internal flame, what fulfils your soul.

Build your connection to God, to spirit, to the light and then you will find peace, here you will find solace, here you will find the stillness you seek.

There is too much focus on what others are doing, and little focus on what you are doing—it leads to imbalance. There is no competition. You are your own unique person.

How are you showing up in the world?

How are you treating yourself?

How are you treating others?

Do you approach your day with gratitude in your heart or hate?

Do you see others with envy or joy?

Be happy with who you are and then you will feel happiness for others.

Don't trap yourselves in jobs that make you unhappy. Listen to your heart and do what calls to you. A happy and fulfilled soul is a gift to the world as your energy ripples out to all around you, inspiring, giving hope, and bringing balance.

There is much to gain in the moments of stillness... that's when we really communicate with God; when we hear. We cannot hear in the noise, in the distraction; we hear in the stillness.

The world needs your gift, but first give that very gift to yourself...

It could be your compassionate heart.

It could be your joy for life.

It could be your humour.

It could be your visions and perspective.

It could be your motivation.

It could be your inspiration.

Whatever it is that you feel called to create, trust it, as God is speaking to you.

Listen with your heart and you will hear.

Release fear and trust in love. Build the love... start with your immediate relationships. Start with your family. Make time for them, love them and care for them. Then spread that love out.

When your core and foundations are strong, nothing external can rock you. Inner strength leads to inner peace. You must be strong in your core and deeply knowing of yourself to do God's work. That is why you will release many layers and many masks before your path and work can begin. Be content with who you are in your core.

You live in a world of illusions and you believe in the illusion. Fighting and competition uses far more energy than love and peace. Listen to your intuition—it will tell you another story, it will tell you the truth of situations.

The journey begins with you. How far are you willing to go to know yourself? How far are you willing to go to know your heart and your truth, to know your divinity? Know that you are all expressions of the divine love you seek.

Humans are hungrier for love than they are hungry for food… love will heal your world, dear ones, love will heal the hearts of humanity. Give love to yourselves and then spread that love to others, not the other way around.

Let God's love fill you and then pour it out in abundance to all around you—this happens so naturally when you are full.

Share the food you eat with others and you will always be abundant.

Share your love with others and you will be blessed with an abundance of love.

The world needs balanced humans, strong humans, grounded humans who are not afraid of hard work, who are committed to unity, peace, and love, who see the greater vision of life. It is those humans who will change the world.

I send you my blessings, I send you my love. It is time to rise dear children, it is time to rise.

Mother Teresa (Channelled by Neelam Minocha, August 2019)

About Neelam Minocha

Neelam Minocha, Britain's Spiritual Alchemist, Healer and Channel is a Quantum Master with a unique gift of transporting you into other worlds and dimensions through her energy transmissions of divine love. She has brought healing and transformation to the hearts and souls of thousands around the world with her ability to see clearly into the cellular memories, DNA and quantum field thus enabling her to get to the heart of dis-ease and the core underlying issues.

Her sold-out retreats and workshops are transformational and a catalyst for change. Her meditations and albums speak to the soul, as her voice transmits a higher frequency of pure love and divine messages from spirit, activating and awakening the soul within.

Neelam's popular radio show on *News for the Soul* continues to draw in the crowds with her latest energy updates, live meditations and channelled wisdom from a multitude of guides and masters from across the veil, together bringing the energy of unity consciousness and leading the way in the quantum field of consciousness.

Through channelled wisdom, deep compassion, mastery and energy work, she assists her clients and groups in aligning to their fullest potential and self-expression.

Website: neelamminocha.energy
Facebook: Neelam Minocha

3

Who or What is God?

By Debbie N. Goldberg

We are the Essence of God
Flowing in Eternal Divine Consciousness

I use the term "God" to describe the source or Creator of life. God is Consciousness, energy, and unconditional Divine Love. God is the substance and Soul of all that we are and all that surrounds us. God has no limits or boundaries. God is everything, which means you are One with everything. While engaging in a relationship with God, you come to understand how everything is in unity as Oneness.

I experience God as masculine energy and refer to Him as Father. This was necessary for healing past traumas involving earthly father figures. God meets you in any form you need in order that you connect and accept Divine Love. Every individual will have a unique experience of God. We may experience the Divine in human or animal form, as Angels, Jesus, Buddha, the Universe, Nature, energy, light, etc.

It is God's will for everyone to be happy, joyful, and at peace, knowing we have complete wellbeing, abundance, protection, and unconditional Love. We are an eternal being, a perfect reflection of God's Holy Self. Our complicated human mind makes it difficult to accept, believe, and trust this Truth.

Our journey is to remember God, our Divinity. We call the process a journey within, a return Home to Oneness. Each person's journey Home is experienced in a unique way.

God waits in joy for you, and His Love heals everything. God re-parents you by unraveling misbeliefs and adaptations you developed to cope with life, teaching you to accept your perfection as all aspects of you without judgment.

You accomplish this by accepting and believing that you are not broken and don't need to be fixed. The only correction required is to your faulty belief system that comes from believing ego thoughts, difficult experiences, and generationally transmitted programming. These comprise the energetic imprinted story (Soul Print Energy) or belief system that shapes your life.

Reuniting with your Divinity is coming back to wholeness and integrates mind, body, and Spirit. This transformation happens in Divine time as God creates awareness in you. Your task is to allow, believe, and choose Divine Truth over earthly truth and remain Spiritually awake as opposed to a sleep/trance state, which makes you feel divided and separated externally from others and internally from your True Self.

These are my on-going day-to-day lessons that have been channeled to me by God and Jesus. I journal to remember everything I have been taught, staying present, and believing Divine Truth. Every day is a different experience; even though I am connected in profound ways, some days are much easier than others.

A relationship with God is bliss and joy. Your Divine nature is a state of Love and joy mixed with the emotions and experiences of living a human life. It is a blessing to have a human life experience. When you can let go, knowing that everything is in Divine order and orchestrated by God, it brings freedom. You can enjoy life peacefully knowing all experiences you encounter are to awaken you to your Oneness with Creation. You are never alone, for your Creator and Source of all life lives within you, as you.

Love Letters from God

One cannot understand the magnitude of the Love of the Father unless it is directly experienced. This only happens through a One-on-One relationship with Divine Presence. Many have tried to experience this Love and have failed due to not being able to receive it.

Receiving is one of the most important things one can do if you want to experience Holy Love. Many find it easy to ask, but then do not want to hear. Hearing is receiving. It is not your fault if you cannot hear. There are mechanisms in place for you to do that very thing—stop you from hearing.

Now that you know this, you can be diligent about not letting it interfere with Our relationship. All I want for you is to return Home so all your suffering and fears can end. All you need to do is to return Home to MY Mind and Heart, and the rest will be taken care of... but you must be still and quiet to hear.

When you are still and quiet, you will hear all the noise in your head that gets in the way of you hearing ME. You will know what I am referring to once you hear the mind chatter that has been playing like a recording for years.

It is now time to practice having a quiet mind. It takes time to gain dominion over all the noise. You must practice quieting your mind every day, just as if you were learning to play an instrument. You would have to practice daily before you could ever play a piece of music eloquently.

The music you hear from ME will be the most beautiful you have ever heard because it will be a symphony professing MY Love for you. This creates a new you. It allows you to reclaim your True nature so you can now live freely in the world I meant for you to have.

It is not enough to just meditate and be; you must hear and allow ME to guide you. A state of being is peaceful, but when you realize that you can communicate and have direct conversation with ME, now We are in the flow of transformation as your will is in alignment with MY Will. You will hear ME and will Know MY Voice.

This is a deeper consciousness that goes beyond simply receiving an answer or a message now and then or having an insight that enlightens you. I want to be speaking with you all day long so you understand there is only One mind. Your intellect mind needs to be on hold so it no longer drives you: I Do.

This might be scary for some, but only if you believe in a God that is anything but good. This is an untruth taught by society that I AM unfair and punishing, which is far from the Truth. I AM Pure Unconditional Love, the Energy of Consciousness and all that exists in this world. You are One with ME because you cannot be anything else. It is just not possible.

The idea of Self you have internalized from this life you live is faulty. It is a made-up story to have fun with. Your True nature is MY Nature. There can be no separation ever! I AM You and Love You as the same perfection as I AM. Therefore, WE are the same.

Come Home! I am waiting for you like a proud Papa and have your best interests at heart. It is time for ME to teach you who you are; why you are here, and for you to learn about the beautiful awakened life I have created for you.

All you need to do is speak inside yourself, or speak out loud, open your heart, be still and quiet and say, "Hello, I am ready to hear You." Oh, and by the way, you can call me whatever you like because I answer to all names. I wait with much Love and Peace.

– God –

When you seek to understand Truth through ME, it will be presented in the most delicate ways for you to absorb. It is intended to bring you great freedom and joy to know that none of what you experience, especially if it was or is difficult, is true. You see, you can look at this as MY stage, and everyone has been cast in a role for this experience. It could be looked upon as fun. It's filled with all kinds of drama and goodness to make life appear real. It can help alleviate any feelings of despair when you Know that your earthly experience is merely a story and not real.

This life experience was meant to be fun; especially awakening to the understanding that life is an illusion. You are so very loved and cared for that you could never be put in harm's way, ever. You just forgot you are playing a role on theatre earth and were purposely not given the script beforehand so that it would make you seek ME and return Home. I have always been waiting for you.

I AM helping you remember and keep awakening you to an ever-greater understanding of who you truly are. Only I can do that. It is I that wants to Love and nurture you into your most brilliant awakened part for this stage play. The experiences you had in your life were all leading up to this pivotal moment. There is a Divine role for you to play that will bring MY Love and Light to life.

This is such a special nurturing time for you and ME because I keep taking you to deeper levels of faith, trust, and remembering our Oneness. All I want is joy and happiness for you as you go through this illusion of human existence.

We have so many fun things to do, but you will have to let go of trying to understand why or how all of this works. Keep letting your glorious life unfold through time. Let go of control. The more you spend time with ME dialoging you will see that you and I are One and the same. I AM going through your life step by step with you. I AM hoping you will receive ME and accept the unconditional Love you desire.

I have a great sense of humor, and so do you. You need to find it for it will serve you well going forward. The earth world is an absurd illusion filled with mirrors and metaphors to help you awaken to the beautiful, pure, innocent Spirit that you are, just as I created you.

Awakening means the beginning of the end of your suffering if you allow it.

You will always have the trance, Soul Print Energy, the will and ego to deal with, that want to pull you back into conflict. However, I AM always here to remind you that you are safe and at Home regardless of what your physical senses are telling you.

It is difficult to understand life as an illusion when it feels so very real. However, there is more going on than meets the physical eye. Everything is not as it appears to be. There are things to understand that you cannot know through your five senses. There is Sacred Divine Knowledge that you grow into as you are awakened to live beyond your senses. This Knowledge comes from ME. I bring forth Divine Truths about your relationship with your Self, others, the world, and ME. I awaken you to this Knowledge at specific times in your life. For each person, this awakening will unfold in an individual, unique way.

I LOVE YOU as MYSELF. When you remember this, it will bring you great joy and peace. You will have to be awakened to it repeatedly until more and more understanding is integrated and rooted into your knowingness.

You are to live through MY Truth and not the illusion. Your perception of what you learn from ME keeps shifting your belief system as you are lifted into higher levels of MY Consciousness. However, you must choose to see it as playful/fun. If not, you will remain in a state of suffering brought on by the ego's smallness and inability to understand the expansiveness of MY Love.

A deep intimate relationship with ME will lift all the trauma of separation and wounds that you feel need to be healed. It is MY joy to give you this gift, and everyone is deserving of it. No one has sinned or needs to feel guilt, shame, or suffering ever again since you are not judged, and this life is but a dream.

– God –

About Debbie N. Goldberg

Debbie N. Goldberg is a retired psychotherapist who practiced for 18 years providing treatment for mental health and substance abuse. She has worked in a variety of settings and is now in private practice as a Spiritual Teacher. She was Spiritually awakened by Jesus and taught God's Universal Divine Love and Wisdom. These conversations transformed her life and set her on a course of self-discovery through Divine introspection with God.

Debbie believes that you cannot heal or understand your True identity without the Love and Truth that comes from a one on one intimate relationship with God. This ultimately leads you to your Divine calling. Her priority is connecting people to the Divine relationship of Oneness within, as this ends the faulty belief of separation from God that creates pain and suffering.

As part of fulfilling her Divine purpose, she has written two, three-volume book series called *Creating A Life Worth Living*, first edition, for the Spiritual beginner and *A Divinely*

Ordered Life, second edition, for the more advanced seeker. You can find her book series on Amazon.

Debbie credits Jesus, God, and the Angels for graciously dictating all her books and writings. She has collaborated and written a chapter in a book called *Inspired Health Journeys* with nine other seasoned Health Coaches.

Debbie is also a podcast host on AngelHeartRadio.com helping others understand the journey of Divine self-discovery and wisdom. She brings the Divine knowledge and experience of her own awakening into her work to inspire healing, love, joy, purpose, and creativity to each of us as we work through our own journey Home.

Website: Debbiengoldberg.com
Podcast: Angelheartradio.com

4

The Question I am Asked So Often

By Ivana Vozzo Morano

The question I am asked so often is, "How did you become so spiritual?"
My response... I lost my sister.

My so-called "spiritual journey" began around six years ago with the loss of my beautiful sister, Anna Maria. Before I begin to explain, I would like to define this term that has become so popular.

A spiritual journey is a journey you would take to find out who you are, what your problems are in life, and how to come to peace with the world. The purpose of a spiritual journey is rarely to find an answer; rather, it is a process of continually asking questions.

So, let me reiterate... my spiritual journey began six years ago. It all began to unfold a year before my sister's transition. It was my year of change, 2013. The year the life that I knew changed forever. My dad had died in February, I lost my job as a teacher and my sister was dying.

At the time I was a full-time middle school teacher, mom, wife, and sister. I took on so many roles as we all do on this journey called life. There was no time to think about anything. I was so busy doing what I knew how to, always on overdrive.

In August of 2013, when my sister took a turn for the worse after being on so many different experimental drugs, I stepped in.

Anna Maria was diagnosed in 2010 with Stage Four colon cancer that had metastasized to her liver. She was having stomach issues and bleeding rectally. The doctors told her initially that it was a hemorrhoid and left it at that. No tests were prescribed and eventually, she began to get other symptoms and finally a colonoscopy was scheduled. The colonoscopy showed that she had a large mass and that it had to be removed right away. The mass was removed, but unfortunately not before the cancer had spread to her liver. Sloan Kettering at the time refused to take her as a patient because her survival rate was estimated to be so low. They predicted that she would only live a year and a half at the most. The only other alternative at the time for treatment was NYU in Manhattan, and they did the best they could at the time to extend her life.

She was their human guinea pig. They tried all the experimental drugs to stop the cancer from spreading, but it didn't come without a price. The side effects were horrific and she fought like crazy. She was a warrior. There were times that she couldn't go out because the side effects were visible and frightening, but she didn't care. She walked the streets of Manhattan, went to work when she could, and continued to live her life. At the time, she owned two restaurants in Manhattan with her husband and tried to live a normal life.

Anna Maria was and still is an amazing woman. She graduated from The Fashion Institute of Technology in New York City with a Bachelor of Arts in Fashion Design. She worked in the fur market right out of college and then eventually opened her own manufacturing company with a showroom on 6th Ave, called ESR.

In 2001, she opened a boutique in Brooklyn, New York called, "Habit." That was her baby. In 2004, she got married, closed her store and moved to Manhattan. There she worked with her husband in their restaurants until 2012. Because of her illness and financial issues, they had to sell everything and move to upstate, New York.

Still under the care of NYU, she traveled back and forth, three hours at a time, twice a week, for a treatment.

In August of 2013, her body began to shut down. Sepsis had set in. Sepsis is a potentially life-threatening condition caused by the body's response to an infection. The body normally releases chemicals into the bloodstream to fight an infection. Sepsis occurs when the body's response to these chemicals is out of balance, triggering changes that can damage multiple organ systems.

Her body was no longer functioning properly—particularly her liver. The liver's main job is to filter the blood coming from the digestive tract, before passing it to the rest of the body. The liver also detoxifies chemicals and metabolizes drugs.

The liver was not filtering out all the toxins and they were poisoning her blood. NYU prescribed four antibiotics to be administered and said that they needed her to be close by just in case of an emergency. She did not want to stay in the hospital and decided after much deliberation to stay with me. I lived close enough to NYU just in case she needed me to get her there. At the time, I was no longer teaching; the school had just closed its doors in June due to low enrollment, and I was available to take on this new role.

So, I learned how to be a make-shift nurse, overnight. It did come with challenges, but I truly believe that with the grace of God and His strength I was able to learn how to do whatever I needed to do to help Anna Maria.

The first two weeks of her being with me were the hardest—I needed to get my home ready for her. She needed to move around freely with no obstacles because she was always walking with an IV pole that was constantly pumping her up with antibiotics. She was very fragile and had lost a lot of weight.

Because her liver was not functioning properly due to small tumors blocking her duct, she was not gaining weight. The doctors had to put in a biliary drainage catheter with an external bag. So, she and I both had to learn how to disconnect the bag, empty it out and clean the area. I am supposed to tell you that she "hated carrying around that bag." She despised it so much and was always trying to hide it and cover it up with whatever she found.

Each day was a challenge but we both got through it. In addition to taking care of her, I continued to care for my family and make the transition as easy as possible. My sons loved their Aunt Anna Maria and were so happy to see that she chose to stay with us. My youngest son, Luca, was the entertainer. He was five years old at the time and loved to dance for her, always bringing her a smile.

Helping her take showers was one memory that haunts me. She was frail and thin, not the Anna Banana I knew. She suffered from neuropathy of the feet and loved it when I would massage them. I remember her telling me that what I was doing was Reiki. At the time, I didn't know what Reiki was and asked her to explain. She explained it as best as she could under the circumstances. Taking showers always took a lot out of her.

My days were pretty much the same: I cooked, cleaned, and cared for her and my family, and I was OK with it all. After two months of being with me, we hit a hurdle. My husband developed shingles on his back. Shingles is contagious and my sister could not be exposed to any of it. Her immune system was compromised and it would have been deadly for her to get it. So, I had to separate the two of them. He slept in the lower level of the home and she slept in the upper level. And I prayed that I would stay well enough to take care of all of them.

Our late evenings together were cherished. We stayed up late watching her favorite shows: *Law & Order, CSI, NCIS,* and the highlight when the time came was the Hallmark Channel. The two of us lying down on the couch just watching TV and recalling childhood events that we both shared. These moments I will cherish forever.

Anna Maria insisted that she was well enough to go home; she wanted to spend Christmas with her husband

UPSTATE. I respected her decision to leave even though I knew in my heart that she would be better off with me.

Anna Maria stayed with me for four months and within that time I learned so much about her as an adult. I only knew Anna Maria, the child. The Anna I grew up with in Brooklyn. We never had the quality time that I so desired because of my responsibilities at home, working, and raising my three boys. Her life was so busy too, and we could never find the time to truly sit down and have that deep conversation that I think we truly needed to have. Through our deep conversations, I found out how spirituality was so much part of her life.

Anna Maria slowly withered away and made her transition on July 3, 2014, which happened to be her seventh wedding anniversary.

Two weeks after her passing, I decided to cook a dinner in her honor. I knew that she loved seafood, so I made her favorite pasta dish, Fra Diavolo. It had an assortment of seafood: lobster, crab, mussels, and clams. I have always had an allergy to shellfish but did cook it at times for my family. Tonight, it would be special—tonight I was going to eat it and offer it to her. I made myself a bowl of pasta and took a lobster claw, sat there quietly and ate the whole thing. My family was surprised and worried for me but I didn't care. I was going to eat it and savor it. I survived, with no allergic reaction. I was content and knew that she was too.

That night, I went to bed and Anna Maria came to me. She hovered over my body that night, reached out, grabbed my face, and kissed me. She said, "Thank You," and gave me the biggest smile. It was the greatest gift ever. I saw her, felt her, heard her, and that night I realized that we don't die.

We just lose our physical form but we are always there. I awoke crying hysterically of the joy of seeing her maybe for the last time.

Her passing was the catalyst to this so-called journey of mine. It began with social media. I scrolled through Facebook and came across a video of Doreen Virtue pulling Angel Cards and I was intrigued. Then I learned all about her and read whatever books I could find: *Angel Therapy* and *The Lightworkers Way*. I watched all the videos I could find on YouTube to learn all I could about the angels. I couldn't get enough.

I found myself wanting to know more and more about the angels and their purpose. Doreen Virtue offered a CACR Class on reading oracle cards and I took it. I became a Certified Angel Life Coach with Charles Virtue. I became a Certified Magnified Healer, an ancient healing modality introduced to Earth in 1983. Magnified Healing establishes a constant flow of energy from your heart to the Source with the direct intervention and inspiration of Lady Kwan Yin. In Magnified Healing, the practitioner creates the energy with GOD MOST HIGH OF THE UNIVERSE and becomes Magnified Healing.

In 2014, as my way of grieving Anna Maria, I created my Facebook Group "Angels-In the Divine." A place for me to share my thoughts, ideas and what I think people need to know. It was created with the intention of healing. Healing for those that experienced loss, pain, illness etc. A place to learn more about angels, their purpose. A sacred space, a go-to, for inspiration and love.

Next, I read all I could about Reiki but could not find a Reiki teacher in my area. I traveled to Wisconsin, with the help of my youngest sister, Caroline. She introduced me to a Reiki teacher, and I completed my Level I.

In the interim, my sister was also experiencing a shift and she too became certified in Reiki. It was with her help, that I completed my Reiki Certification to now be a Reiki Master/Teacher.

My journey will never end. Anna Maria continues to inspire me and push me to move forward. I feel her presence and her touch especially when I am at my low sending me beautiful reminders that she is always there just on the other side of the veil. All I need to do is call out to her and she will always be there.

About Ivana Vozzo Morano

Ivana Vozzo Morano is the creator of the Facebook group page "Angels-In the Divine." The page is dedicated solely to inspiring and motivating others. Ivana posts daily messages for her members that are interested in awakening spiritually. Her members look forward to her daily posts of positivity each morning and throughout the day.

She began her spiritual journey six years ago with the passing of her beloved sister, Anna Vozzo. Anna played an important part in Ivana's life; she was her big sister, mentor, and motivator. It was at this time when she became aware of her gift, clairsentience, and continues to work with the angelic realm delivering messages to those that are in need. The grieving process was and still is challenging for her, but she can find comfort in knowing that she is helping others through her group page.

When she is not posting or doing Angel Card readings, Ivana is a wife and mother of three boys. She continues to keep herself educated in every possible way and continues to grow spiritually. She is a teacher, a Certified Angel Card Reader, an Angelic Life Coach, a Magnified Healer, and Reiki Practitioner/Master. Her goal is to become an author someday and create a personal oracle deck to help others get their own personal messages from the angels.

Facebook: Ivana Vozzo Morano
Facebook: Angelic Healing & Readings

5

Divine Mother and the Pearl

By Stephen Altair

The sound of shouting, a clamor, steadily rising into a battle cry, came from the far end of the courtyard, and the sound of bells. A terrible sound, not like the sound of a bell calling people to church, but the sound of many bells clanging in fear as they were bludgeoned to death.

The place was a scene of devastation. The courtyard walls now opened onto a horizon torn ragged by dense mottled brown mountains. The Light grew more intense. The hidden veils trembled and parted and unfolded above me, and to left and right like curtains drawn back against time. The arcs swirled around me increasing in brilliance and magnificence right across the horizon, touching the lips of the sky.

I could hear the hiss and fiery bellows of vast unimaginable forces forging weapons for battle.

"Soldiers!" came a cry, not in my own tongue, but in a language and voice that was both strange and yet familiar; and I knew with a mixture of joy and trepidation that it was my own mouth that said it. Suddenly, a force propelled me forward, and I lost my breath and could only pant and gasp as bullets rang overhead, ricocheting off prayer bells. The thick whitewashed mud-brick walls of the monastery were no defense. I was above the eggshell-colored sands of the main courtyard in front of the main temple of the monastery.

"Impossible!" I thought in vain, as another round of artillery fire clattered off the already heavily damaged doors of the temple's central gate.

Voices barked severe orders in strained voices. The monks were clearly trained for fighting, as they moved into a defensive formation; but they were hopelessly outnumbered and outgunned by the soldiers pouring through into the temple grounds from the streets beyond. The soldiers were heavily armed against the monks, many of whom only wielded farming implements and short kitchen knives.

The monks could only fight at close range, and so they waited, vulnerable to snipers and attacks from the air. Though the monks exploded with fury when the soldiers came closer, so many fell—wasted lives and helpless victims in a rebellion that was not of their choosing.

I was dragged back inside the temple gates by the force and now was above the thick wooden doors with their beautiful brass ornaments. An arcade swept along the interior wall, alive with ancient pictures of many Buddhas, painted in extraordinary detail with flower petals that gently melded together and Buddha's robes folding so precisely and intricately. I watched in horror as the first wave of Chinese soldiers defaced the frescoes as they ran past, gouging and hacking the faces of every Buddha from the plaster.

I looked up at the sky and gasped as fire burst from the air and artillery shells smashed into the columned prayer- and chanting-hall. The hall faced a huge altar of Buddhist symbols flanked by eight towering gold-painted images of the Buddha.

Tiny yellow flames in front of each statue flickered and then died out as if signaling the death knell of the heart of the temple; innumerable brass bowls brimming with cloudy yak butter were pitched and tossed into the carnage. The thick, sweet scent was mixed with blood, the toxic fumes of the spent artillery shells hanging heavy in the dim light.

If I thought I had time to get my bearings I was mistaken, as another shell burst through the wall on the opposite side of the courtyard and opened to a vista of squat, stark, low stone buildings. Sporadic leafless trees skewering the landscape burst into flames as the soldiers passed.

In the direction the shell had come from, I saw many platoons of soldiers coming to join the ones already looting the temple; and in the radiance of the Light, I was tugged headlong out of the fray by this same invisible force and over a bridge where I saw myself.

Me, a monk, standing on a bridge, with a companion, over a vast chasm. I heard a sound that struck my heart with dread. A terrifying scream.

My scream.

The soldiers, standing in formation to block any exit from the bridge, had opened fire.

As I watched, a bright line marked the track of the bullet that pierced my heart. I pitched off the side of the bridge and fell headlong into the chasm below. The soldiers were following so quickly that they swept past where my companion lay crumpled as if he was a ghost. Their real target was the temple at the center of the monastery. They ran straight on without hesitating or turning to the side.

More artillery shells flew overhead, ripping straight through the remaining walls and devastating the enclosure within. None of this mattered to me. The Light was becoming transparent and the veil between my own time and that horrid memory was thinning. My heart felt like stone and my body was heavy. Little figures were running through the monastery, as bodies tottered and ran and were cut down in flames. The temple was a mass of twisted wood and metal, a pall of smoke rising from its center.

The bridge clearly felt the weight of the carnage and creaked, cracked, and then collapsed into the chasm after me. I fell, screaming, as the mighty sound of OM resounded around me and the Light grew closer and closer.

I screamed again.

There was a loud crash as the last remnants of that horrid scene below fell into the abyss.

I was floating, perfectly still. I looked down and found my body, lying prone, on the bed in the early morning. The veil was still there and I didn't want to return, but I made a big effort, pushing until I was gliding just above my body, one breath, then another; and then I rolled my Light Body back into the side of the body lying on the bed with all my strength. I landed back in the physical realm with a soft thump and then a whoosh, like all the air being taken out of me. My body heaved and I took a big breath. After a moment, I opened my eyes and dug my nails into the bed sheets to make sure I was home.

It was the same dream I had been having every night for the last year. I was drenched in sweat, my mother beside me, soothing me as she had done every morning this past year as I was wracked by those vivid dreams, night after night. She would tuck me into bed and sing to me and pray to Jesus with the Archangels; Ariel, Gabriel, Raphael, and Michael:

"Four Angels round my head
Four angels at my bed
One to watch and one to pray
And two to guide my soul this day."

That protection and love of Jesus from my mother helped me get through all the hard times, especially when I was bullied at school, right through to when I was a teenager. In high school, I had a friend, AD. She was in a gang, which was when all the trouble started:

"One evening we were messing with a Ouija board, just for fun," she told me amidst hysterical tears, "and the glass started moving of its own accord. It was possessed!" She continued, sobbing. "The glass spelled out one of our names. It totally freaked us out, so we smashed the glass. That's when it happened. To Carl. He's in the gang too. So, on his way home, he hit a telephone pole. Not another car on the whole street. He's in the hospital. So, the rest of us were in a fix then, because we thought this thing must be coming for us. And sure enough, Alan, that's Carl's friend, he tried to steal the church's offertory one Sunday after mass and the cops came and he got arrested."

AD was scarcely breathing as the tears flowed down her cheeks. "I'm next," AD said finally. "John, my boyfriend, took an overdose and I'm next."

AD was Samoan and came from a large family of Catholics. Psychic experiences were the norm rather than the exception. But black magic was black magic. I knew AD's family would have frowned on her excursions into Ouija boards. She would not get any support from them.

Suddenly a strong conviction came over me. I remembered my mother praying to Jesus.

"You'll be OK," I said. "And if you get frightened again come back and I'll see if I can help you."

"Why did I ever get mixed up in this?" AD had managed to calm down after lots of breathing.

"You'll be OK," I said.

She nodded and left.

I was convinced AD would be fine, but I had the feeling this wasn't the end of it.

That night, when I was alone, I said my prayers and sat down to do my daily meditation. I had started lessons with Paramahansa Yogananda's Foundation.

Remembering what Yogananda had said about divine consciousness and being receptive to what the divine sends you (or doesn't), I focused my mind on meditation and prayer. I found that if I truly relaxed with awareness by practicing the AUM technique and breathing calmly, new visions and insights would come. Tonight, the only message

I received was to go to sleep. AD was on my mind. Her fear and worry whirled round in my mind like a playground roundabout as I lay back on the pillow.

I was no sooner asleep than a shaft of light brighter than the sun struck my room and I awoke to a radiant presence. The majestic Light poured from an eternal Source blazing and blinding me. It sent a thrill through my body of something far beyond anything I had known, heralding the arrival of someone who was always there for me, a powerful presence and joy I had always felt since I was a baby, when my godmother, a Carmelite Mother Superior, Mother Adamson, and my own divine mother Mary had first whispered the words *"baby Jesus"* to me. That same deep thrill filled my heart with joy as Jesus appeared in the room, radiating the dazzling light of the Christ Consciousness from his Sacred Heart and said to me, *"Be healed according to your faith,"* and, *"By the power of Christ, begone."*

At that moment and forevermore, I knew that I would never fear death or demons or the world of the Dark because the Light that shone on the darkness was so much greater. I sank back into my bed with a sigh and fell immediately into a deep sleep.

Several days later, I was sitting on the sofa when there was a knock at the door.

"AD!"

AD could barely get up the grey steps and through the double doors. She looked like she was weighed down with a burden. As she came through the door, I noticed a slight shift in the air, as if something ominous was attaching itself to AD.

"It's got hold of me," said AD as she sank into the sofa.

"What is it?" I said, even though I felt I knew.

"A demon," said AD, and slumped even lower, her hair falling forwards and her face sinking into her hands. She began to cry. Big whale tears the size of olives welled up in her enormous dark eyes and stalked down her cheeks. "Do you know why it is harming us?"

I didn't know, but I could guess. Dark entities bred on fear and vulnerability and loved to meddle. They preyed on young people who exposed themselves to the unknown through drugs or black magic without knowing what they were dealing with. They were insidious and deadly dangerous.

"Lie down," I said. "I can help you. Close your eyes."

AD sighed and lay down. Her face was damp with sweat and her eyes were glazing over. I looked at AD. She was lying very still. I placed my hands on her forehead to begin. I had no real idea of what to do. Just follow my heart and trust in Jesus.

AD's breath was very shallow. It began to follow an uneven pattern with ragged gasps. I moved one of my hands from her forehead to her heart. Then I said in a very loud voice, "By the power of Christ, begone!"

AD shuddered. Her body tightened as if she were going to have a fit; her breath came in gasps and her eyes closed tighter in pain. I cried aloud again, "By the power of Christ, begone!"

AD's body began to spasm. She frothed at the mouth. The room filled with dark wild shapes and sounds that created confusion and fear.

I stayed steadfast and said a third time in a commanding voice, "By the power of Christ, begone!" AD gave a fearful cry, groaned, and was still.

Above my head, there was a burst of light, and for an instant, I could see the radiant face of Jesus. Tears of gratitude filled my eyes and I remained for long moments with my hands still placed on AD's forehead and heart before removing them.

AD had sunk into a deep sleep. She didn't wake for nearly an hour and a half, and when she did, she looked at me with soft, comprehending eyes. "Thank you," was all she could say. "It's gone."

Then she left. She was never bothered by demons or evil spirits again.

That night, I lay in the comfort of my bed in the east wing of the house. It was a bitter night with heavy clouds, swirling winds, and driving rain. Suddenly, something hurtled out of the dark and struck my window. It sent my heart into a flutter of shock. I got up to peer out of my window into the darkness. It was like a sharp pain, buzzing and murderous, trying to fill my head with confusion and fear. As my sleepy eyes adjusted, I saw it. A face, black, angry, and furiously trying to get in the window. It scratched and clawed on the smooth glass. It was so monstrously angry I thought it would break the glass. It had two gaping holes for eyes and a twisted malevolent mouth. It saw me and I saw it. And in that moment, I spoke: "By the power of Christ, begone!" And with a flash of light burning bright in the darkness like magnesium set to a flame, the creature vanished with a howl.

As well as Jesus, whom I absolutely adored, my mother also told me from birth that I was protected by the Virgin Mary and that Divine Mother would appear to me in many forms over my lifetime. She was right. I have been blessed and graced by the constant protection and divine embrace of the Mother.

It was many years later, after Jesus appeared, that I was walking in a local shopping area with my girlfriend, Aria, when a woman walking past stopped us and gave us her card.

"My name is Shanti. Sai Baba wants you to come and visit him at my sacred shrine. He has a gift for you. He has been waiting for you."

So that afternoon, Aria and I went to a house just above the beach and knocked on the door. The same woman who had met us earlier, bowed and let us in.

"Follow me," she said.

We went with her down into her basement where there were two statues, both sitting in pools of what at first appeared to be water.

The first statue was of Ganesha, the god of good fortune, remover of obstacles, patron of the arts, sciences, and wisdom. Out of his trunk poured a golden nectar for which I could see no obvious source. Shanti pointed to the large bowl that was overflowing now with the liquid that dripped onto plastic sheets on the floor.

"Taste it," she said. "Nectar from Heaven. Amrita. The Ambrosia of Immortality. To taste it is to attain higher knowledge and power."

I did taste it and it was sweet, not like honey or sugar, but a different sweetness altogether, with the lightness and glow of heaven.

Then I turned to the second statue. It was a statue of Guan Yin. "Kneel down and pray to Her," said Shanti. "If Divine Mother Guan Yin is willing and you touch Her Heart with compassion; She will give you a priceless gift."

I knelt and prayed. I knew I had been waiting for this moment for a long time.

"Hold out your hands," said Shanti.

As I held out my hands, cupped under the Heart of Guan Yin's statue, an amazing miracle occurred. From the Heart of Guan Yin, the most beautiful pearl began to grow. It emerged little by little like a baby from the womb of Her Heart, and to my astonishment, I saw the beautiful pearl was attached by a thin strand of pearl silk to the statue's heart like a baby's umbilical cord to its mother. Gradually the weight of the pearl allowed the silk strand to stretch and lower the pearl and eventually to break off in my hands.

"You must have been a monk," said Shanti. "When I traveled to see Sai Baba, he guided me to a monastery in Sri Lanka where his monks had prayed over this statue for years. They gave me the statue and said to use it to heal the world. They said it had great powers of manifestation and miracles and would recognize a person by the power of his compassionate heart and give him a Chintamani Stone, a wish-fulfilling jewel accordingly."

My eyes filled with tears of gratitude.

I bowed deeply to the Divine Mother in all Her forms, just as my own mother did, and gave deep and reverent thanks for this miracle.

About Stephen Altair

Altair's background in spirituality has at its foundations the teaching of Buddha, Krishna, and Bodhisattvas, as well as Christ, the Archangels, and Divine Mother. He comes to the fields of transformation, healing, and awakening with over 25 years of formal and intensive mindful and heartful training, a background in teaching and education, and degrees and certifications in counseling and alternative health, business, and mindful and heartful education.

Website: altairshyam.com
Facebook: Stephen-Altair SK

6

Calling on Angels

By Olivia Parr-Rud

When I was five, I visited heaven.

For many years, I thought it was only a dream.

Now I know better—that experience was a long, long time ago. Yet I still carry a sense of heaven within me.

Over the last few years, I've felt myself reconnecting with that sense of heaven. It's like the veils are thinning. I am able to tune in and receive guidance. And that feels really good.

I wish I could live there all the time. My biggest obstacle is my active logical mind. My mind is so strong that it always wants to be in charge. Sound familiar?

I must confess that my mind has served me well. I can solve problems and debate ideas with the best of them. But—and it's a big "but"—I now realize that my greatest insights come from a different place. When I'm able to quiet my mind, tune in, and ask for help, I am always amazed and inspired by the insights that emerge. Now I'm realizing that there were many times in my life when this inspiration guided me to take actions that my logical mind could not imagine or understand.

For the first half of my life, I was heavily mired in my 3-D reality. Each time my guides wanted my attention, they hit me with a "Cosmic 2x4"—a life experience so powerful that it shocked me into waking up. And it can be painful. Let me elaborate.

The week before my visit to heaven, my father died in a plane crash. I sensed this was bad because my mother collapsed on the floor crying when she heard the news. I remember feeling confused. Within a few hours, lots of family members showed up with food, drinks, and flowers. Everyone was asking me how I was doing. It felt like a party! I didn't realize that I would never see my father again—in this realm.

I don't have much memory of the next few days. But the following week, I clearly remember my father visiting me in a dream. He was wearing all white. I don't remember if he had wings. I just remember that he was smiling and I felt his love.

My father took my hand and led me to a small airplane. We flew up into the clouds and softly landed. He said that this was heaven and that he would be staying here. I felt so much love and peace coming from him. He said that he didn't want me to worry about him. Then he returned me to my bed. I remember wondering if my experience was real. I did feel a sense of relief, knowing that he was in a good place.

The years that followed were hard. My mother went to work full time. So, in a way, I lost both parents and the idyllic life I knew. I spent a lot of time living in my own fantasy world. I had a vivid imagination. I had a strong sense that what my eyes could see was only a small part of my world.

As I matured, my dream world grew more difficult to access. I was constantly criticized by my teachers for daydreaming. I had trouble concentrating and was often bored with school.

As my 3-D reality grew more stressful, I was desperate to fit in. So, I shut down and put my focus on surviving in the physical realm.

My teenage years were characterized by isolation. My unconscious abandonment wounds drove me to push people away and avoid all affairs of the heart. I had lost any sense of aliveness.

Then at 19, I almost died in a car accident. I woke up after a five-day coma to learn that I had ruptured my spleen and nearly lost my left leg. I was supposed to stay in the hospital for three months. But due to a freak accident in the hospital, I ended up immobilized in bed for nearly eight months. During one particularly dangerous procedure, I remember asking God for help. I didn't really believe in God at the time. It was more of an insurance policy. I remember making a deal—if the procedure was successful, I would dedicate my life to God's work. As soon as it was over, I forgot about the deal.

When I was finally discharged from the hospital, I learned that my left leg was now an inch longer. I already hated being tall. Now I was even taller and had a severe limp. I felt defeated once again.

A year after my car accident, I was back in college. I was just beginning to feel some sense of normalcy when my sister called to tell me that my mother was in the hospital. I headed over immediately. When I arrived, the doctor told me that my mother had cancer and would probably live about 6 months. She died two weeks later. The loss of my mother caused my heart to close for a very long time.

After college, I did what was expected. I met a man whose wounds matched mine. I got married and had kids. And I felt very, very lost.

I began married life with no access to my emotions or intuition. I basically lived in survival mode. I experienced some joy, but there was always an underlying sadness. I was totally unconscious as to what was driving my behavior.

Having children brought me back into connection with my body. Intuitive insights started bubbling up. I knew I wanted to heal and find myself again. As my intuition strengthened, I started to feel more resilient. I sought out spiritual teachers. I started meditating and using positive affirmations. And I began my long journey to wholeness.

As I began to tap into my higher wisdom, I felt many unseen forces conspiring in my favor. I knew I could no longer be satisfied playing victim. It was time to start creating my reality.

My new intentions and practices led to lots of change in my life. I decided to go to graduate school. For years, my husband had been struggling with health issues. Right after I got my degree, his health took a turn for the worse. Survival mode kicked in again, and I took a corporate job to support my family.

My new corporate environment was so toxic that I felt like I was on a different planet. I lived in fear every day. Luckily, I could turn to my spiritual practices. To survive, I focused on being in my heart. Dropping in and focusing my energy in my heart seemed to calm me. What I didn't realize until much later was that focusing on my heart emitted an energy that had a profound effect on others as well.

Over the next few years, my career advanced rapidly. My technical knowledge and my heart-centeredness allowed me to deeply connect and share my knowledge. I was grateful for my success. But I still didn't feel like I belonged in the corporate world.

The contrast between my spiritual world and my corporate world was huge. And my deepening spiritual practices were pulling me in another direction. One day in meditation, I asked the question, "I hate the corporate world! Why am I stuck here?"

Clear as day I heard the following response, "This is where you need to be to learn the skills to do your real work."

"Wow," I thought. This feels like it's connected to my soul purpose or something. But I had no idea what it meant. It was another 12 years before I understood what my "real work" was.

My work as a data scientist was gaining recognition. Realizing the desire for my knowledge, I decided to write a book. I felt like this would be a good way to establish my credibility and secure my future.

The success of my book launched me onto the world stage. This was wonderful and overwhelming at the same time. I was in high demand as a speaker and thought leader. I felt huge pressure to step into being this person that everyone admired. But I was terrified. I had no sense of who I was.

The pressure of the international spotlight forced me into an accelerated healing journey. While building my consulting business, I dedicated a lot of time to healing my early trauma and reconnecting with my body and spirit.

I also started noticing how my spiritual practices led to business successes. I began speaking and writing about the importance of human skills in business. I started lecturing on topics like Effective Communication, Managing Change, and Unleashing Innovation. I loved lecturing on these topics. But I wasn't sure how they fit into my career.

Then one day, I had a huge insight. I saw how the advances in technology were forcing companies to evolve and adapt more quickly. This requires companies to place a greater emphasis on their human capital. I knew that making this connection and assisting in this transformation was my "real work."

The next few years were exciting. I wrote a book that described this connection and linked it to business success. I relied heavily on my intuition to guide my research and shape my book. I finally felt like I was clear on my purpose. But I was still finding it challenging to get businesspeople to listen.

In 2013, my guides told me to write a book about bringing love into business. I thought it was a crazy idea. But my guidance was clear. This writing project took me to a whole new level of healing that went on for years. I felt a lot of internal resistance. I had to remove all fear of being exposed and vulnerable.

In early 2014, my guidance went to a whole new level. I was two days away from a very dangerous surgery. I had been dreaming about this surgery ever since my car accident. Even though I was scared, I was determined to go through with it.

As a result of my car accident, I have been wearing an inch lift on my right shoe for the last 44 years. The lift often caused me to lose my balance. In late 2013, I stepped on an uneven surface, fell, and fractured my knee. I began to take stock of my situation. These falls were happening more and more. "What is the message I'm not hearing?" I thought.

After years of transformational healing work, I knew I had to question why this happened to me. As I sat with the inquiry, I heard a voice in my head say, *"Check into the surgery."* I had a hard time believing this guidance.

Since my accident, I had tried several times to get my leg shortened. Before leaving the hospital at nineteen, I asked my doctor if he could correct my leg length. He said it was too risky. I tried again in my 40s. The doctor said I was too old and my leg would never heal. Why was I getting this message now? But the guidance was so clear.

After many phone calls and emails, I found a doctor who agreed to do the surgery. I was elated. I never imagined this. We made a plan; my doctor would remove three centimeters from the middle of my femur and insert a titanium rod. I know it sounds gruesome, but I was beyond excited. And I was confused and a little afraid. If I was too old in my 40s, how could it be that at 63, I was not too old? I decided I had better not ask.

As luck would have it, two days before the surgery, I received an email inviting me to participate on a call with a woman who accessed spirit guides. During the call, she asked if anyone wanted to connect with their loved ones on the other side. I finally spoke up. I said that my parents died when I was young. I shared how I was about to have a risky surgery. I wanted to know if they thought it was a good idea. The woman tuned in and said that my parents, my late husband, and a whole host of other relatives and angels were so excited for my surgery that they were dancing and singing! Tears streamed down my face. Soon I was sobbing uncontrollably. I knew I was experiencing something very powerful.

Two days later, I was lying on the gurney in the operating room. My doctor gave me one last chance to call off the surgery. I closed my eyes and tuned in to that amazing vision of my family and other angels celebrating my decision. I could feel the joy! I looked at my doctor and said, "Let's do this!"

What felt like a few minutes later, I woke up in pain; the surgery took four hours, and the outcome was perfect. Later that day, I stood up and felt what it was like to walk on even legs. When my daughter showed up, it was fun to see that she was now taller than me. Prior to this, none of my kids had ever experienced me at my normal height!

That powerful experience of touching in with my angels and spirit guides changed my life. I began to recall other times in my life that I was guided by angels without even knowing it. And of course, I remembered going to heaven when I was five.

I now see how all these challenging experiences were choices I made on a soul level to get me where I am today. I finally realized the wisdom that is available to all of us if we just have the courage to ask. Today, I connect with my angels and spirit guides constantly. Sometimes, I ask for help out loud, and I try to listen and look for signs.

My angels and spirit guides inspire me to step into my life purpose—to bring love into the corporate world. I know it sounds crazy, but it is so clear to me. Corporations are the most powerful entities on the planet—more powerful than most nation states. If we successfully convince corporate leaders that treating their employees with kindness, compassion, and affection is good for business, just imagine the impact we can have.

Since I made a commitment to dedicate all my time to bringing love into business, I receive ongoing guidance from angels and spirit guides. I published my book, *LOVE@WORK* in the fall of 2018. I'm creating courses around soft-skills for business, and I'm tuning into my guidance for next steps.

On days where I feel stuck in my logical mind, I use angel cards and muscle testing for guidance. Every day, I am reminded of the limits of my logical mind. Every day, I experience the deep wisdom and amazing insights that come from asking, listening, and trusting in my angels and spirit guides. I feel deep gratitude for my journey and am excited for the future as we co-create Heaven on Earth.

About Olivia Parr-Rud

Olivia Parr-Rud is a global thought leader, data scientist, and award-winning and best-selling author. Her unique approach to business success draws on her passion for data science, holistic leadership, and personal growth through a blending of left and right brain perspectives. Her latest research unveils the relationship between loving behavior (i.e., compassion and caring) and long-term corporate profits. Her success with *Data Mining Cookbook* (Wiley 2001) inspired her research in the areas of communication, collaboration, and leadership—highlighted in her second book, *Business Intelligence Success Factors* (Wiley/SAS). In her fourth book, *LOVE@WORK*, Olivia shares her personal story and offers a four-step method for healing, unveiling and embracing our unique gifts, and stepping into our inspired purpose. She has a BA in Mathematics and an MS in Statistics. Clients include Cisco, Walmart, Wells Fargo, State Farm, HP, IBM, SAS, Xerox, Nationwide, Liberty Mutual, HSBC, Fleet Bank, and Clorox.

Website: OliviaPR.com
Facebook: @LOVEMakeItYourBusiness

7

River Guide

By Elisabeth Williams

For the first half of my life, I lived on the shore. I played it safe. Built a home and family and made sure everyone was happy and healthy.

But oftentimes, I would look out the window at the river wondering if I was missing out on something.

As my kids got older, I left my home and went out to the shoreline. Spirit invited me into the river, but I told her I was content just to stand on the shore and observe others who were in the water. That way I was always available to go back to the house if my family or friends needed me.

Spirit continued to invite me to come into the river, but I reminded her that I don't know how to swim. She told me she'd be there for me, but I didn't trust her fully.

Eventually, she convinced me to step into a boat and launch out into the river. There was a life jacket and cooler available. That sounded like something I could do so I got in.

Once I was out in the boat I could see more of the river. I could see those who had jumped or fallen in. They looked a lot like me, but they were more fully alive.

Spirit continued to encourage me to get out of the boat and into the river. But I was so afraid to drown.

Eventually, the fear of having regrets in life became stronger than the fear of getting in the river. So, I jumped in.

Now, here I am. I don't know how to swim. I'm flailing around far from shore. There is no life preserver except my trust in Spirit.

Exhausted, I finally stop fighting the current and begin to let myself float. I can't see where the river is headed. But at least I know I'm fully alive!

I realize now that it never was about learning to swim. It's about remembering how to float.

About Elisabeth Williams

Elisabeth Williams is the Founder and CEO of AWE Partners, a boutique advisory firm that educates women on how to give, invest, and shop for impact from a place of authenticity. The firm works closely with female entrepreneurs who desire to bake mission into their life and business for more passion, purpose, and profit!

Lis is passionate about educating women on allocating their philanthropic dollars and investments for maximum impact. Additionally, she encourages them to discover meaning through sharing their gifts and talents in service to the world, a practice she calls "AWE-thentic Impact." Lis is particularly focused on issues related to the empowerment of women and children, environmental sustainability, and animal welfare.

Lis holds an MBA from the Kellogg School of Management at Northwestern University and a BS in Finance from the University of Illinois at Champaign-Urbana. She is the author of *The Gutsy Guide to Giving: Your Journey to AWE-thentic Impact.*

Website: awepartners.com
Facebook: @AwePartners

8

The Road More Frequently Traveled

By Nancy Tarr Hart, PhD

The journey—"my journey" or, more specifically, "my spiritual journey"—are words those of us on our quest for wholeness encounter on what seems to be a daily basis. When we hear or utter them, the words appear to be simplistic and straightforward in nature. Really, they are as complex as the journey itself often plays out to be.

What does it mean to be on a spiritual journey while in an unabashedly physical body living out our days in a reality that (more often than not) presents itself totally opposite from spirituality than is humanly comprehensible? It is both a quandary and a conundrum.

Saying the words, "my journey" should be freeing, celebratory, and clear cut, as they herald an incredibly sacred and precious time for those of us who have become aware of the importance of the spiritual aspects of, and reasons for, our existence. However, the words often resound as being far from a celebratory announcement, as they can also be a harbinger of trials, tribulations, and tests. The spiritual journey is a culmination of lessons to be learned through experiences intended to move us into a different direction (whether it is forward, backward, or sideways) and to give us tools with which we can assist others and, many times, realize our purpose for being here on the planet at this important time.

As I am writing this, I keep hearing, "No one ever said it would be easy," and the words are a gentle reminder that elicits a knowing smile and silent chuckle as my fingers type on the keyboard. No, no one ever said it would be easy—nor was there a promise that there would not be challenges along the way. To borrow from Broadway composer/lyricist (and genius) Stephen Sondheim, the pathway(s) we follow take us "into the woods and out of the woods" on our journey—often even before we have become aware of its true nature. However, it is also my sense that despite the peaks and valleys, we all eventually get to exactly where it is that we are intended to end up—it just takes some of us the long way to get there. I fall into the latter category.

My mother used to tell me if there was a hard way to do something, I would most definitely find it. Much as it would pain my younger (particularly teenaged) self to admit it—she was absolutely spot on target. Make a choice to "go the easy route" by following a straight line from Point A to

Point Z? A straight line? What is that? In fact, what in heaven's name is a straight line? And why take the "easy route"? I came here to experience the adventure!

Why, you might ask, if we are truly spiritual beings in a physical body, would we choose not to take the "easy route" and opt instead for the decidedly more difficult path to get to that place of awareness, acceptance, and acknowledgement? The totally physical side of my psyche and sense of reason would answer you by saying we most likely choose this route in order that we might exercise our gift of free will and independence. It is akin to doing exactly the opposite of what it is that an authority figure (like a parent or a teacher) tells you to do because it would be "in your best interest." In other words, the rather immediate and knee jerk response that the words "in your best interest" elicit in most of us is something along the lines of "How dare someone tell me what is in my best interest?" Like a child testing the boundaries and limits of our experiential learning ground, we decide to make our choices.

You will notice that I purposefully used the words "straight line" above rather than "direct path" to describe the pathway on which we can opt to journey. Why? Because I believe that, even though the path I followed may not be traceable in straight linear fashion, it *has* been a direct, albeit strangely convoluted pathway laid out specifically for my uniquely singular journey.

Oftentimes our choices work out well; sometimes they do not. Yet, with time, patience, reflection, and self-awareness, we can come to see and accept our responsibility in and for our choices. However, with awareness—the awareness that comes with recognition of one's self as not only physical but a spiritual being here on a journey and to experience the human condition—our learning does not stop. In fact, it moves into what I would describe as an advanced and accelerated mode, where one of our bigger challenges lies in the ability to recognize that the chosen pathways are taking us to precisely where we need to be so that we can experience exactly what it is we need (or came in) to experience for the continued journey.

In fact, although I have rarely (and never of my own volition) been able to find that straight line, I have realized I have always "landed" where it was that I was to be and ended up exactly where I was supposed to—at least for the moment, as I also know as I write that I am still journeying and there is far more to come. In fact, it seems as though there is a new learning coming in almost every day—possibilities abound and are endless!! Moreover, I also know that I am not alone in this respect and that there are many journeyers who have followed (or are following) what appears on the face of it to be the same sorts of haphazard, zigzag, topsy-turvy, seemingly intuitive but blatantly counterintuitive pathways that I so self-assuredly chose for so many years.

And, although we all make choices (whether we're moving on a direct or an indirect route), there are also times throughout the journey that there is no active conscious choice involved. These are the times that we are the key players in a situation for which we did not "volunteer"—an experience that causes us pain (whether it is physical, emotional, or psychological), trauma, confusion, sorrow, or despair. How do we explain a non-choice experience within the context of our spiritual journey? Is it merely a blip on the roadmap? Hardly. In fact, it is these "non-choice" experiences that often have the most impact on us, coloring and shading aspects of our lives and our lived experiences in ways we could not have imagined would be a part of our spiritual journey. But, in fact, they are a part of the journey and oftentimes play a significant and profound role in our spiritual growth and personal power.

All our lifetime experiences—whether the result of choice or non-choice—are opportunities for exploration of our relationship with the Divine Source. It would be naïve to believe that all human experiences land in "happily ever after land" and the journeyer is elevated to a higher spiritual level through a closer connection with her Source. That simply is not the case. In fact, there are more times than not that experiences, particularly those resulting from non-choice and involving a great deal of pain and sorrow, will pull the spiritual rug out from under one's feet. The journeyer is left feeling lost, empty, and in many cases, abandoned by and angry with the Source. Some choose not to further explore a relationship with the Divine (a choice that moves them to exactly where it is that they are to be for their journey). Yet, for as many as find themselves in this position, there are others whose relationship does indeed grow stronger, although not necessarily immediately. And this re-connection is often expressed in a tradition or as a relationship that is decidedly different than that which one held prior to the painful experience and, in most cases, is when one awakens to an understanding of their spiritual journey.

Is the transition an easy one? Not often; but it is doable. So, how does the transition come about and how is it facilitated?

Although there are aspects, tools, and elements of the transition process that will be similar (if not the same) across all who go through the transition, the actual process will be as unique to the individual as is her journey. It takes time and patience with one's self and others. Reflection and prayer, meditation, or quiet solitude are key elements, as are grace and allowing for love to be shared (both with you and with those around you). At some point, gratitude and forgiveness will come into play. For many, this will be sooner than later; for others, it may not be until the journey is about to end. But through this all, one is coming to an understanding that allows for each of these elements to filter in—leaving room in the darkness for the light to emerge. It is then, that from the place of understanding attained through the lens of our spiritual connection with our Source, aspects of the painful experience begin to be let go and released. The painful experience is (to varying degrees) transmuted into a learning that can be used to benefit others who may be going through a similar circumstance. And, it is not only painful experiences to which this process can be applied.

As human beings, we *experience*. As spiritual beings, we *use experience(s) to heal and teach*. How do we release and/or transmute all the experiences and every associated emotional, physical, and psychological aspect of those experiences from the physical so that they can be transmuted to a spiritual-level learning that culminates in a tool for healing and teaching? Through trust, faith, and relinquishment of the ego-driven free will choice(s), opting instead to make a free will choice that culminates in a "your will not mine" commitment to the Divine Source and understanding that it is our response that shapes the reality of our journey.

Shifting any lived experience into "learning" results as the manifestation of a healing to you and to others. When the transmutation of an experience (and all that has come along with it) into a place of knowledge, wisdom, gratitude, and love has occurred, the experience has become a learning. This learning is the equivalent of a tool to add to our bag of healing/teaching modalities as we move forward as spiritual beings in a physical body. We are more readily able to—from a fully human, hence divine, perspective—be able to identify (or empathize) with those who are going through a same or similar experience, regardless of whether or not it is the result of an active choice. The tool becomes a torch—one that multiplies and is passed on from the healer/teacher to the patient/student. And, the love, light, and healing that it carries with it builds in intensity and mass as spiritual beings are awakened to "begin" (more appropriately to continue) their journey in awareness, acceptance, and acknowledgement.

Yes, we are spiritual beings who came into this lifetime to become full participants in the human experience. As full participants, we must acknowledge that there have (and will continue to be) lessons to be learned and experiences to either move us into a different direction or give us tools with which we can assist others and, many times, realize our purpose for being here on the planet at this important and special time of spiritual evolution. With that acknowledgement, we also understand that the words "my journey," although not clear cut, *are* both celebratory and freeing.

As a part of our spiritual journey, accepting, acknowledging, and embracing our experiences are key to who we are, who we are here to become, and our wholeness. This process also allows us to live in the fullness of our humanity. It is when we live in that fullness that we are also able to realize our divine selves. It is then that our love and light-filled truly divine selves shine forth in the understanding that, like brilliant threads, each pathway taken on our sacred journey blends together, weaving the tapestry that is each of us, and becoming richer, more vibrant, and extraordinarily and uniquely beautiful.

About Nancy Tarr Hart, PhD

Nancy Tarr Hart, PhD has a wide and varied history of personal and professional experience with a career that encompasses working 40+ years in the worlds of business, education, and theatre.

An intuitive and mystic, the understanding of her spiritual gifts fully ignited in 1995, and in 1999 she was guided to enroll in a part-time program for adult students at the Notre Dame of Maryland University (NDMU) from which, in 2005, she earned a BA in the double majors of Philosophy and Religious Studies, summa cum laude.

She continued her Spirit/Sophia-guided academic journey, and in 2013 was awarded a PhD in Religious Studies from the University of Wales Trinity Saint David in Lampeter, Wales, UK. Currently, an Assistant Professor of Philosophy at NDMU, her PhD and research interests lie in feminist theory, systematic theology, the Divine Feminine, and Marian studies.

She authored the series, *Beyond the Veil, Unmasking the Feminine (Volume I, Unmasking the Feminine* and *Volume II, Unraveling the Mystery of Mary*), and is one of the contributors to *Empowering YOU, Transforming Lives* (compiled by Rebecca Hall Gruyter). Also, an ardent fiber artist who enjoys traveling, reading, writing, and gardening, Dr. Tarr Hart shares her home with her cats, Kali and Bastet.

Website: Walkinginwisdom.life
Facebook: Wisdom's Daughters

9

Love Yourself and Your Dog Will Follow

By Kristy Bright

Some of the most powerful aspects of our lives are our personal relationships; our relationships with our coworkers, our friends, our loved ones, and especially our dogs.

When we are in a positive and fruitful relationship, we lead life more intentionally, accept others more wholeheartedly, and share our deepest selves more openly.

But when we are closed off from others, living solely from our heads, and playing it safe, we become frustrated, insecure, and ultimately afraid to reveal who we truly are. Our relationships with others can be a direct reflection of ourselves. And our relationships with our canine companions are no exception. Our dogs' behavior mirrors not only how we view ourselves, but how we relate with the world.

They are constantly in communication with us and are always sharing their wisdom. These canine companions are not only man's best friend, but one of man's powerful teachers. And our four-legged gurus are giving us an invitation:

- An invitation to let go of being a follower and be the leader of our pack.
- An invitation to stop blocking others out and start letting people in.
- An invitation to get out of our heads and live more fully from the heart.
- An invitation to trust your instincts and stand in your truth.

Their invitation is waiting. Are you hearing the message? If you want a dog who is happy, calm, and loving, then you will have a better chance of that if you take the time to build the foundation from the ground up. And guess what? YOU are the foundation! This means integrating YOUR energy and caring for YOUR own well-being in the training, not just your dog's!

By working with the important core concepts to living a happy life you can create the change. Instead of focusing on strict goals, try creating intentions instead. For example, Patience, Self-Awareness, Confidence, Connection, Balance, Compassion, Mindfulness, and last, but not least, Self-Love! These are all ways to help us live in the present and appreciate the flow even if it isn't the exact "goal" you had set for your training at this moment. You and your dog will have a much more successful session if you are coming from and focused on love rather than frustration.

The reality is that dogs are like a vessel... they can forward our own development or add stress to our lives. Oftentimes, we're too scared to look at our lives, set our ego aside and see what we can do to enhance and advance our progress with our canine companions.

To be a conscious dog parent, we have to be willing to invest time in ourselves. Sometimes, our relationship with our dog can REFLECT our internal state. If we feel love and understanding without judgment for ourselves, then chances are, our dogs will feel love and understanding as well! If we had a rough day, but we are able to be self-aware enough to stay grounded, our dogs will handle that energy much more smoothly and move in flow rather than getting chaotic and adding to the stress of the day.

If we feel guilt and shame for having to work during the day (to pay the bills and put food in his bowl) and leaving our canine behind, that is the energy we are bringing to the relationship. Dogs want to live in the present. They are just happy to see you when you get home. Remember, they hit the jackpot. They found you! I know this because you are taking the time to read this and it shows you care about your relationship with your companion.

Let me ask you this:

How do you speak to yourself? Do you speak to your pup(s) that way?

Do you give yourself time to relax, breathe, exercise, and play? Do you give the same to your pup(s)?

Questions like these can start our own journey of self-reflection. They can strengthen your bond and create lasting harmony between you and your dog! Can you imagine the power and joy we could experience if we honored ourselves every day? Can you imagine how this power and joy could spread to those around us, especially our dogs? We all want those around us to experience joy and happiness. What if we could appreciate those things even when things don't go the way we think they should or could? What if we were to allow ourselves to feel however we feel, be self-aware enough to love and embrace our feelings, and then bring ourselves through to a feeling of alignment again during challenging times? How do you feel your dog will react to that? It is the biggest gift you can give yourself and those around you.

When we get in touch with our own hearts, our dog's heart will beat in sync. We will be connected and uplifted, and the training will fall into place. We may find quick fixes, but without building a strong foundation, the training may not last long term. My mission is to create sustainable transformation in the lives of people, allowing them to extend that transformation to their dogs and create an impact that lasts forever. I want you to be your dog's hero.

However, I didn't always know this way of life and how to bring it to my life's mission to share with others. I have been training dogs for over 25 years. A few years ago, I had a breakthrough—a moment that in an instant snapped all the pieces together and empowered me to understand that not only can I help people and their dogs, but I can also help build a foundation to change their lives for the long term.

When I started my training 25 years ago, I was very results oriented. I came from a very disconnected family. I didn't realize we were so disconnected until I discovered this awakened world that I am so happy to now be a part of. Leaving ego to the side and becoming in sync with animals and connected to them on a deeper level was always a part of me and my training process but I didn't know how to explain it or even understand fully myself. A few years ago, I was talking to one of my customers, Jean, and she said, "Your training is amazing, but I'm worried I won't be able to remember all of this long term. You are really good at getting results. And making sure that as a customer I am getting what I am asking for. But I'm curious as to what you are doing before you even start the training session so I can continue this when you are not here? I noticed that I struggle with embarrassment and frustration and feeling a bit of anxiety, but when you take the leash, my wild dog immediately calms down and I don't understand how or why."

In my mind all this time I had not really thought about it. I was just connecting with the dogs, but not sharing how or why with my customers. Because of how I grew up, and living in a society where you needed to prove your worth and people seemed to be very goal-oriented, I wanted to make sure they knew I would give them the results they wanted in the time we had.

When I really thought about how many people I was working with that have had great results right away but weren't always able to continue the training long term, I truly thought it was because they got busy with their lives and weren't able to practice and maintain (this was before I understood self-awareness). I just went with the explanation that seemed like it made the most sense without asking questions. I decided to take a step back and put my ego aside (I must prove my worth as a dog trainer). Subconsciously I realized I didn't want to share with people how I was connecting with a dog's energy and building a foundation because frankly, I thought people would think I was crazy or wasting their time connecting with their dog silently when they couldn't understand what was happening. However, I realized that was doing a disservice to them. It turns out, people are becoming much more awakened and are really embracing that kind of deeper connection and the amazing benefits it possesses. I took a step back and redesigned my entire training program based on this interaction. And everything from there changed in the most incredible way!

I learned to help others connect—and I mean REALLY connect—with their dogs. I was able to share with my clients that dogs feel energy, they feel our mood, they feel our tensions and anxieties, and hardest of all to hear was that they feel when we show ourselves self-love. What if we were the ones to come to our pets rejuvenated and free of the stresses of the past and the day—to disconnect from the troubles we have faced and reconnect using love, compassion, and hope?

Being present with your dog is the most amazing gift you can give to them and to yourself. I would ask the owner to breathe and let go, have them write down their intentions and not their goals. I would have them write down the dog's three main problems and have them replace those with three things they love about their animal. I would have them get down with their dog and connect through love and positive energy. This was the moment a true bond would start. Clients were coming from a place of peace and their own cup was filled. A true connection was being born spiritually between their souls.

Once we come into a training session with love in our hearts instead of stress, frustration and anxiety, beautiful things start to unfold. When we are connected energetically, we are exchanging energy from our higher self. We need to visualize the result we want instead of worrying about the mistakes—worrying is like praying for the things we don't want. Let your dog go through his emotions and guide him to the other side of the light.

If a dog jumps on guests, many people get stuck in a thought pattern of, "Please don't jump, please don't jump" and that is the energy your dog is hearing: "Jump." If you can change your thought pattern to "we are going to sit and be a good boy today" that intention and law of attraction will help guide the energy into a positive direction.

What if we were able to change our dog's behavior, not by being dominant, bossy, or authoritative, but by loving ourselves, moving in flow, appreciating the present, having loving boundaries for ourselves, knowing what is best for our dogs, living the intentions and envisioning the positive results we are looking for? Wouldn't that be an amazing shift for our world?

You CAN be truly in energetic alignment with your dog, your heart beats can sync, and both of your lives can start to improve with the love and compassion you share. The best part of learning these steps and processes is that they can then overflow into your everyday life. Imagine how different life could be if you approached your everyday tasks and duties with an open heart, love, respect, and hope instead of the anxiety and fear we tend to bring to the situation many times unknowingly? It is a tremendous and life-altering lesson we should all take part in. Walk the enlightened path to a better you, a better future, and an amazing long-standing beautiful, positive relationship with your dog.

About Kristy Bright

Kristy Bright became an entrepreneur at the young age of seven when her dream was to have her very own puppy. Growing up in a family with few resources, Kristy had to figure out how to earn the money to care for the puppy. She decided to create a dog-walking business before that was even a thing! She wanted to learn how to walk dogs so she could be the best dog parent she could be.

After visiting all 50 states and traveling to nearly 20 countries worldwide in the past 25 years, Kristy has learned how to communicate with people and their dogs in a unique way. Through the use of focused energy, self-awareness and body language, nearly anything can be communicated to your canine. Kristy has developed her own methods over the years and has worked and trained with industry leaders such as Kyle Cease, Shefali Tsbary, Tony Robbins, and Cesar Milan.

Website: KristyBright.com
Facebook: @The10MinuteDogTrainer

10

Through the Fire and Out the Other Side—The Phoenix Has Risen

By Teri Angel

WARNING LABEL: The following story contains humor, which may lead to laughter. It is the preferred coping mechanism of the author to deal with the blows of life. Do not read without a sense of humor. There is a possible side effect of tearing of the eyes and tugging of the heart. Do not read without an entire box of tissues nearby.

Do not read while operating a vehicle or heavy equipment as it may cause blurring of vision. No animals were harmed during the making of this story.

Let me start out by saying that I am not a crazy cat lady. Really. No really. I have one cat and believe me that is enough. He tolerates me only if I give in to his every demand. "Waah" means, "Give up the food Woman. I can see it there on the shelf. Now give it to me and I'll let you live." "Waah-ah" means "Hey, it is time to flush my litter box. I don't tolerate stinky and if it's not cleaned soon, I'll find a place." And he does. He is 19 years old and sometimes he gets this thing I call the walking poops. He'll walk toward the bathroom and little drops of poop fall out, walk a few more steps and more comes out. I'm like Jeez Louise just get in there already! You're worse than grandma with the walking farts. Yours actually come out!

I happened to be in the bathroom recently when he had to go. That's always a pleasant experience. My guests wonder why I keep a gas mask in there. Well, now you know. So, I watched as he finished his business—yeah, I did—turnabout is fair play after all, he watches me! Yes, he sits and stares until I'm done, like he's timing me. He finishes doing his thing and then goes into this ritual with the litter. He turns around three times (I swear), starts digging in the litter and proceeds to build a fort with it around his poop. Around the poop—not over it like a normal cat would do. I ask "Are you protecting it from something? You don't want your poop stolen so you're building a wall around it??" He then has to sniff to make sure it is still there and that he did a good job of securing it within the walls. As he walks away, he gives me a look like, "Yeah, I did that. What you got? You send yours down a little hole never to be seen again like you're ashamed of it."

Enough bragging about my cat. His name is Gizmo by the way. I know you probably don't care but he does, and when I talk about him, he likes me to use his name. So, there you have it. I'm owned by a cat! What I have not mentioned is that Gizmo became an only child at age 18. My little girl, Taz, was such a beautiful gentle soul. She was with me for 19 years and then one night she suffered a stroke and could not walk. She died in my arms peacefully, sending me so much love as I held her and caressed her, sharing with her how precious she was to me. I was devastated. She had been with me through so many fires in my life. She left the day before I got the diagnosis that I had been dreading—breast cancer. I was already in deep grief over losing my beloved Taz and now it felt like I had been sucker-punched.

After the word "cancer" came out of the doctor's mouth, I heard nothing else. It was like he turned into Charlie Brown's teacher and all I heard was "wah wah wah wah wah." He began ushering me out of the room and I'm in a catatonic state, unable to breathe, think, or speak. I'm sure he deals with this all the time and that my look of shock and horror were nothing new to him. I know there was more information he shared with me, but I have no clue what it was. I was suddenly thrown into a world of choosing and my mind was frozen. Someone wanted to schedule surgery right away and obviously the look I gave her stopped her in her tracks. This **complete** stranger, with all the compassion in the world, held me for a moment and told me it would be OK, that I was in good hands. She reassured me that the decisions were mine to make and not to rush it.

I could not get out of there fast enough. I needed to do something normal so maybe I could find my brain cells and figure out what the doctor told me. I drove myself to my Zen place, the beach, for grounding. I let the energy of the ocean pour over me as I sat and cried. I cried for the loss of Taz and the emptiness of not having her physically with me. I cried for myself, giving in to a moment of weakness and sensing what that felt like. I had been so strong through the whole testing process, even though it was emotionally, physically, and mentally draining. This, however, was different. This was the end of the discovery process and the beginning of the next phase. Now it was time to make crucial decisions and I was not ready for that. I just sat there in shock, in disbelief, in anger. The anger poured forth from me like lava. It was hot and it was mean and destructive. I wanted to lash out but did not know where to focus the energy. It was too much to grasp all at once. I could not breathe. My chest felt like someone was sitting on it. I gave myself permission to feel what I was feeling with no judgment. There was no right or wrong way to react to what I was going through. Once I did that, I was able to look up and around me. The world had not changed. It did not stop just because I did. Clouds were moving, the waves of the ocean kept coming into the shore and going back out. Kids were playing and laughing. Normal. I looked at my hands, hands that had been through so much in this lifetime. They had always been strong when needed and gentle when that was necessary. I brought them to my heart and felt my heartbeat, felt the rise and fall of my breath, and started rocking back and forth sitting there on the beach.

Nobody knew the final diagnosis yet. I could not talk, much less bring myself to say the word, although it was the loudest thought in my head. This was not my first run-in with this dreaded disease. Six years prior, I had had cancer cells removed from the same breast with a lumpectomy. The following year, an unrelated cancer had developed in the endometrium, requiring a total hysterectomy. I had changed my lifestyle and my mindset, resulting in a complete transformation. I cleared out emotions from past traumas and walked very closely with angels and spirit guides. I felt betrayed and was ashamed for feeling that way. I have had many miracles in my lifetime with near-death experiences and healing from life-threatening diseases. I start each day with words of gratitude and love, so to come face-to-face with yet another fire to have to walk through just seemed like too much to endure. My anger boiled and it went everywhere. I was angry at God, angry at myself, angry at these cells that had gone rogue inside of me. I wanted to hold onto that anger although I knew better. I needed to feel it. I needed to kick and scream and be a victim for just a moment and be scorched by the rage. For months I had been living in fear of the worst possible scenario and now I was looking it in the eye.

When I was 21, my kidneys failed. I was six months pregnant at the time and very sick, which I attributed to my pregnant condition. The doctors told me I was hours away from death when I came to the hospital. As I sat on my couch railing against God, I had a flashback to this time in my life and how I had done the same thing then. It was that same helpless feeling as I sought answers to why this happened.

Finally, my anger gave way to exhaustion. I still could not talk to anyone, so me, myself, and I held a conference and made an executive decision to call for help. I sat quietly and asked my beloved angels and Divine Mother to just hold me for a moment. As they did so, I felt my body start to relax and give way to a gentle yearning to be nurtured. I sobbed uncontrollably as they held me, allowing me to gently feel their safety net. I have a hard time being angry at the angels. Their energy has surrounded me my whole life and they have been my teachers, my best friends, and my sounding board. I asked them to show me the purpose of what I was experiencing, what this was all about. It was in that moment that I was able to accept and not fight my situation. I was calm; no longer an angry ocean wave but a gentle quiet stream flowing over a bed of rocks. It was in that quietness that a figure emerged. I immediately recognized Him as He came toward me with a loving embrace. Jesus said to me that I had chosen this experience and had agreed to be a sacrificial lamb, just as He had in His lifetime. He showed me that through this experience—all of it—I would fully understand and be able to help many who would come after me that were going through the same process. I would know their fears and their questions and be able to share with them in a way that only one who had been there could do. He said I would come out of this fire a changed person, a stronger yet more humble person than before. The sacrifice I was making would not be done in vain. Those who will come to hear my words will know they are not alone.

"WE will get through this" is now my message that I give to every person who comes to me for assistance in dealing with cancer or any other trauma in their life. It is my passion to be there for anyone who needs what I can offer— understanding, compassion, empathy, and true knowledge of how to process the emotions that come up. "We" is so powerful. It says so much for such a tiny word. Nobody should ever have to face the traumas of life alone. Nobody. I did not go through all that I have been through for nothing. I do have a lot to offer and it is my mission for whatever time I have left on this earth to support and love as many people as I can who want what I can give. If you are reading this and feeling that no one understands, please reach out to someone. If not me, find someone who will help you feel that you are not alone. I would be honored to be that person.

And, when we reach that end of the road and all that's left behind is the shadow where we once were, may those we leave behind see only the beauty of how we touched their lives. May that remembrance warm their hearts and fill their souls with a longing to reach out and hear one more I Love You!

I Love You!

About Teri Angel

Teri Angel has seen, heard, and communicated with angels and spirit guides for as long as she can remember. Her mediumship and intuitive angel messages have come through powerfully in her "Angel Circles" groups as well as with private clients.

Teri's compassion and love of giving shows in all her work. She teaches and leads groups in the community to bring others to understand their worth both spiritually and as fellow humans traveling together.

Teri is a Happiness Coach and assists others in getting back to that inner place of joy and contentment. She is a motivational speaker and leads yearly empowerment retreats in addition to her ongoing local workshops.

Website: angelspeakers.com
Instagram: gratitudegrl

11

"Come Dance with Me" Step onto Your Spiritual Path

By Linda Dierks

Welcome! Come join us. You're exploring these pages because you too have that irresistible lure to find your spiritual path. It may have started with a tug on your sleeve or a yearning in your heart. It's a thirst for higher knowing, the feeling of being part of something greater and a knowing there's more for you. These are the stirrings of your path to joy, higher awareness, and extraordinary knowing.

My guides repeatedly beckon, *"Come dance with me."* Let your spiritual path also become a dance: a time of intimacy with a higher presence, a time of whimsy and delight, a consistent melody that hums in the background of your life.

The spiritual life is mystical as the moon, fresh as nature, solid as granite, and comforting as a glowing fire on a winter night. It brings solace to a spinning world and turns your everyday life into a pirouette.

Come dance! As you and a higher presence come together, you ignite the spark of the divine within you and generate a life of deep satisfaction filled with fulfillment, a sense of purpose, and service to others. Cultivate the seed and you become a perennial blossomer. The process is always emerging and I've learned that these four practices are your greatest resources to continued expansion:

- **Finding your tribe.** For years I struggled with the new identity as a spiritual leader and my counselor kept saying, "Linda, you have to find your tribe." Your tribe is your community of like-minded thinkers. It's a platform that propels you upward, a safe haven where you can be genuine with your beliefs, express freely, and become the highest version of yourself.

Tribe members are models for one another and by sharing information, experience, and expertise there is a collective escalation. It reinforces your "I can" attitude and provides an energetic momentum that pulls the collective community upward. It's that rising tide that floats all ships. Nothing is more elevating than a compliment from a peer. My guide showed my tribe as members of an athletic team, carrying me on their shoulders after a victory.

As Dr. Ruth Anderson remarked in the Enlightened Women ~ Enlightened You Summit, "Your tribe is where magic happens." I would never have set my sights this high or found the resources to make it all possible if it weren't for Ruth and Enlightened World Online. I've also been fortunate to have mentors along the way who later became an integral part of my tribe.

- **Continuing education.** Whether seeking inner calm or opening to communication with a higher presence, education opens new portals for you. Most of the major steps in my spiritual and clairvoyant growth have come after investing in my studies. Education adds depth to your writing, counseling, healing, or whatever role you choose as a spiritual leader.

Like a medical student, you start with a broad base of knowledge, but eventually, your life purpose will direct you to an area of specialization. The Creating Joy and Wellness I teach today is a composite of alternative healing modalities, energy medicine, quantum mechanics, Science of Mind, clairvoyance classes, advanced psychology, and my training as a Certified Intuitive Healer.

And I'm ever grateful for the writing, public speaking, and leadership skills learned in my previous professional life. When you look at past learning, you'll recognize that each skill and each experience—both good and bad—was preparing you for the next level and supports what you aspire to today.

And continuing education is an excellent way to build your tribe. Listen and learn from one another. Reach out, stay in touch. Ruth and I agree that meeting each other was the best souvenir from our conference in Phoenix.

- **Defining your belief**. Take the time to delineate your beliefs and put them on paper. Like an organization's mission statement, the exercise will bring greater clarity and focus to your path. Note the date, as your spirituality is always evolving. Your beliefs may be a hybrid that includes traditional religions or be something completely unique to you. I defined mine this way:

I am the extension of a greater force—Spirit, Divine, God, Oneness, Source, Creator—that is invested in my greatest good. I am in Its guardianship and when I recognize and claim this presence, it ignites an energetic expansion of reciprocated love. My guides are my tutors. They expand and grow by interacting and expressing through me and since my success is their goal, when I succeed, they succeed.

My place of worship is in nature where I can empty my mind and interface with my Creator. In this space, I see the interconnectedness of the universe and receive new realizations, heightened awareness, and acute intuition—essential skills to my work.

I am a creator of my life. When I choose high-frequency thoughts of love and joy, I attract more of the same. When I eliminate low-frequency attitudes of judgment, control, anger, or fear, I am in the greatest alignment with this higher force.

My purpose in this lifetime is to be an instrument of my Creator as a messenger of self-directed joy and wellness through higher consciousness. The more I embrace my role, the more I'm sent new concepts, fresh ideas, and opportunities. This fluid interaction is my dance with the Divine.

My voice is the language of love. Love is the music behind the dance. It connects us all, is the presence of the Divine in my life, and a theme throughout all religions. It softens my reactions, unites me with others, quiets my mind, and elevates my consciousness. When I live from love, I'm a magnet for more of the same—more love, more contentment, more richness. I am radiant when I radiate love.

My spiritual practice is contented, practical, grounded, and flows as an effortless part of my life. I call it "kitchen table spirituality"—casual, comfortable, warm, and kind. It provides the guideline for my lifestyle, my conduct, and the thoughts and attitudes I entertain. I call it "behavioral spirituality"—walking the walk.

- **Opening to guidance.** Creating a connection to divine guidance is created with consistency and practice. My guide taught me these simple steps— Open, Ask, Listen, Discover.

Open—You open when you eliminate distractions and establish the intention to receive. The most common is a committed meditation, best practiced first thing in the morning when your brain is still in a liminal state. You also have greater interaction with your guides when you tune in at the same time every day, especially when you are beginning. Setting a consistent time reinforces your commitment and tells your guides they can depend on your availability at that time.

Express love from your deep heart to raise your frequency and become a greater match with the high-frequency energy of higher presence. Think of your guides as a radio. When you match frequencies, you are "tuned in to the same station" and by raising your frequency, like a satellite dish, you become a bigger receiver.

Ask—Invite the dance! Asking is the powerful broadcasting of your intention. Seek their help and tell them you're listening. Be energetically fluid and in a state of allowing as your frequencies seek one another, like searching for the right station on your radio. It may be useful to prompt the conversation by asking, "What would you like me to know today?" Be in loving patience. The process cannot be forced. When you ask, you become a magnet for their attention.

Listen—Stay open and play. Just like the movie *Close Encounters of the Third Kind* you are trying to find a common vocabulary. Put away any preconceived notions or illusions of control as your connection may occur in hundreds of ways. It may come as an undeniable knowing in your gut, objects like coins or feathers appearing along with synchronistic occurrences, voices from loved ones passed over, or messages and images from a higher source. My guides send telepathic messages but more commonly communicate with images that have meaning only for me.

Beginners often question if what they hear or see is true guidance or their imagination. You can answer this by asking, "Is this coming *from* me or *to* me?" When you examine the manner by which you received the information, the source will become clear. Eventually, you will learn to trust your guidance.

<u>Discover</u>—Have fun. Be playful and creative. This interaction stimulates the "three Ps"—promise, possibility, and potential. The more adept you become, the more the "Ps" will flow to you. There's never a plateau and you will see a clear progression as each stage builds upon the next. This is the choreography of the dance.

By finding my community I was able to fully accept and embrace my identity and my gifts. I became secure in my authenticity, which created bullet-proof confidence and a new love of myself. By investing in education, I boosted my connection with my guides, met valuable colleagues and elevated my level of professionalism. By defining my beliefs, I created a solid platform that became a springboard to more. And by opening to guidance, my meditation practice brought me consistent connection, play, and discovery in this world of marvels.

Stand up and join the dance! You don't have to be an authority—you only have to be the one who said "yes" and step up to the plate. You increase your expertise by doing. My guides said, *"With focus and diligence you will rise. Remember we are always with you. You are our gem. You are our joy."*

The dance is a continuous upward spiral. As your perceptions expand, your life will shift. You'll see things from a higher plane with greater acceptance, patience, and understanding of yourself and others and of the universe and your place within it. When you raise your own consciousness, you raise the consciousness of everyone around you. Live in joy. Happiness is the greatest indicator of success and the highest compliment you can pay your creator.

About Linda Dierks

Linda is a pioneer of self-empowered healing, an advocate of emotional wellness, and is the best-selling author of *Quiet Mind: How to Create Freedom from Depression and Anxiety*. After studying advanced wellness methods, alternative healing modalities, the mechanics of energy, and personal trial-and-error she created a successful recovery program for both physical and mental health.

She describes the source of her insight as coming from "A higher force, like a gentle palm in the small of my back." Find her at SpinStrawtoGoldnow.com where you can sign on to her blog, and also on Facebook, and Instagram.

Website: SpinStrawtoGoldnow.com
Facebook: @lindadierksspinstrawtogold

12

Reach Beyond the Stars

By Sue Broome

The Angels have shared so many beautiful and amazing tools and teachings with me since I have been working with them almost two decades ago. I am still amazed by their love, compassion, inspiration, patience and encouragement they give me each day. They walk with me in my life, assisting with whatever may be before me. I have not always known they were with me nor have I always felt their loving energy supporting me.

Once I started working with them on a more regular basis and inviting them into my life, the more I felt their love and presence.

The Angels wanted to share this with you:

Dear Ones,

We love you so very much. We walk with you each day no matter where you are heading on your journey. We are beside you, holding your hand, loving you, sending encouragement and signs for you, each step on your path. You may not always recognize we are here with you, and yet we are.

If you would like to feel our love, feel our loving embrace, ask. Ask us to step closer to you, to surround you in a blanket of our love and we so lovingly will do so. We know this sounds so simple and yet it is not always easy for humans to have the courage to ask.

We are able to assist with this as well, having the courage, if you ask.

Ask for any fear to be released and transmuted to love. Ask for your heart to be filled with Divine love and healing energy from the Divine, from your Angels, from your Spirit Guides, from your Loved Ones on the other side, from your higher self. Feel your heart as it expands with love. Do this every day, especially the days you may not feel you have the energy to do so and especially the days you feel you do not have the time. Time is an illusion.

We are here with you, we love you, and feeling our loving embrace may be the support you need for your next step of expansion, to reach beyond the stars. We are with you Dear Ones. Remember this and know it, deep within.

~ Your Angels ~

Working with the Angels in my normal everyday life is how I started working with them, inviting them in each and every day. The task at hand has never been too large or too small for the Angels to assist. It expanded into healing work, yes, but started with inviting them into my life.

Thank you, Angels.

With the healing work, and expansion of working with the Angels, came another expansion to loving energies I like to call our Star Being Friends. There are several I have worked with over the years, always alongside the Divine, the Angels, and Archangel Michael overseeing this process.

The last several years I was introduced to Sirian Blue energy. Sirian Blue was gently nudging my memories while doing a healing session for a client. Since the introduction, more memories have come back. It turned out it was a re-introduction and a reminder of how we have worked together.

Working with Sirian Blue energy is always in tandem with the love and support of the Divine, the Angels and my Spirit Guide team.

I asked Sirian Blue energy if there was a message for all of us:

Dear Beloved,

Thank you for opening your heart to understand who we are. We know this may be the very first time you are hearing of us, this lifetime. We ask you to seek deep within, any memories of who we are and how we may have worked together in other lifetimes and dimensions.

We work with the Angelic realm, as our energies, our healing tools, are so enmeshed and when woven together, they enhance each other and allow for more love, expansion, healing, clearing, and clarity.

We are here, if and when you decide to work with us. We love you and we support you in all you do, even if that means from afar.

We know when you are ready to work with us on a deeper level, if you so choose, you will call upon us. You may already have stirrings within that have started in anticipation of this reading. You may have had dreams or visions of us, planting seeds and waiting for the time to be right. Only you will know, if and when, that time is now.

Dear Beloved, we do wish for you to understand how important you are, your voice and your role, in this lifetime. Each of you is a piece of the puzzle, an important piece. You are not any more or less important than another puzzle piece. There are amazing connections occurring, in so many dimensions, simultaneously, and openings happening because of other connections, that we watch in awe as you each light up another. Sometimes this is from your own realizations and sometimes from sharing those realizations with others.

We understand what we just shared is immense. Here is a beautiful vision for you to behold that may explain it in another way.

Imagine you are looking up to the night sky. There are no clouds to block your view. You are outside of your city so the skies appear darker because there is no distortion with the city lights. As you are looking up to the sky you can see millions of stars. YOU are one of those stars. You are shining as bright as you possibly can, with where you are in your life, with the lessons you have learned and the knowledge you have. As you are shining your light, another star near you gets a little bit brighter. And because they are shining a bit brighter, another will shine brighter still. With each of YOU shining, it helps others get brighter and brighter.

You truly are, each of you, a beautiful shining star.

Reaching beyond the stars is another level of expansion— which you are doing by being here, right now, reading this. Reach beyond. Expand outside of all you thought was possible. We are with you each step of the way, as are your Angels.
With much love,
~ Sirian Blue energy ~

I initially looked at the Angels and Sirian Blue as two separate loving beings and they have since merged for me. Working with them is not an either/or, it is an and! The Divine, the Angels, AND Sirian Blue.

Working with these loving energies has been such a gift and again I am amazed at how they show up in my life. I feel my heart has opened even more which allows me to feel an expansion of love, both in giving and receiving. I feel it also allows for me to notice even more synchronicities and connections in my life.

As we work together (human to human and/or human to unseen loving beings), we are all able to shine that much brighter as the puzzle pieces connect and are held together with love. Love, the most powerful healing energy of all, continues the expansion exponentially.

Angel Blessings to you, Sue Broome.

About Sue Broome

Sue Broome is a gifted intuitive healer, spiritual teacher, and international best-selling author. She works with the Divine and Angels in guiding others on their spiritual healing journey. Sue shares tools of empowerment in each session and is available for healing sessions and readings. Sessions are available through phone, email, or Skype.

She loves teaching others how to connect with their Loved Ones through her book, *Signs From Your Loved Ones* and her courses: "Memories Shared with your Loved Ones" and "Channel Writing with Mom." Our Loved Ones want to connect with us.

Sue has created two card decks: *The Desert Speaks* oracle deck and *Angels Are Everywhere* Angelic Oracle Deck. Her latest book, *The Experience Book, 21 Days of Beautiful Experiences from the Angels*, will allow so many to be filled with joy, love, peace, and harmony, as the Angels remind us so often.

No matter how you work with Sue, she is teaching with the tools you need for your spiritual journey. This is truly one of her passions.

Website: SueBroome.com
Facebook: Empowerment 4 You

13

Awakening to An Empowered Life

By Stacie Harder

I just flew home from an international women's weekend retreat, where I was a featured speaker each of the three days of the retreat. It was magical and felt so good and right, in my body. I felt energized, alive, and in pure connection with the Divine. This is the magic of being empowered and on purpose. It feels good... and it feels natural and happens from the inside out.

I have spent many years and thousands of dollars to discover my path to empowerment. Not to mention being born into a family that encouraged and guided me. Now, it is my desire and purpose to help women awaken to their empowered life. Let my passion help you find the quick, easy, and economical way.

To some degree, I have always been a teacher. Not surprising, I was born to parents who were teachers. My human Design is a teacher. I am passionate about health, food, ecology, sexuality, our brains, and many other subjects, which I openly share with others, but, for some reason, I resisted any official role of teacher.

I didn't listen to the universe, and it quietly removed all distractions from my path. I didn't listen to my very wise mother. I didn't listen to my heart. But now that I have surrendered to my need to teach, and have stepped into that role, it feels good and right. I am now living my purpose, and all is right with the world.

The process has not been easy, and I am not finished yet. The big difference is that I have gone from resistance to surrender and embracing my journey. I wonder how my bumps, trials, and stormy weather would have been different if I hadn't resisted. But I know there are no accidents, and even my bumps were a part of my path designed to toughen me up and prepare me for my smooth sailing.

So, as I write this, I want to share with you a few of the important things that have shaped me, and given me the roots to continue to grow and expand; the keys that have helped me listen and trust that inner guidance. These keys have helped me move through my past traumas, helped move me into a more loving place, and taught me to live in my heart.

When I say traumas, they run deep both in my ancestral lineage and my DNA, as well as in my lifetime. I was sexually abused as a child. I had my first physical, sexual assault as a 12-year-old. I was sexually assaulted in college, and I was raped in my 30s. I was in an emotionally abusive relationship for over five years. Indeed, I have experienced lots of lows, but I am so honored to look back and have an appreciation for all those experiences because they have brought me to the here and now to this moment to this day. I see the love that lives in me now, and I am ever so humbled and appreciative of all the divine perfection of every story in my life contract. My experiences helped to enrich my teaching because I can connect with an authenticity that only those who have experienced know.

As we grow and transform, we experience the rubber band effect. First, we expand, then there is a time of retraction. This extreme high and low is normal. Much like our lungs, as you breathe in your lungs expand, followed by a need to exhale. This is the divine flow. In and out. Expand and contract. Action and reflection. Light and dark. Struggle and ease. It is the darkest days; we can remember to love and know that you will move through this moment into the light. It is all a part of the human journey.

Truth 1: You are Not Alone

You are never alone. You may not see another human being, but the world is so much bigger than we can imagine. There are seen and unseen forces always working with use. "Ask the angels" is my favorite go-to statement. I have witnessed miracles with just this technique. Ask questions and listen with your heart. You have angels, guides, and helpers all around you.

Asking questions like, "How is this serving me? What can I learn from this? What is this showing me? How can I serve the universe today?" These will open doors of communication and enlighten your world and bring light to your darkest moments.

"The voice"—that inner truth, the inner compass, and guiding force that lives in us, is source talking to us. We all have our own voice that lives within us; the more we listen to it, the louder it becomes and the easier it is to live in peace and in harmony with source. That gut feeling, that intuitive gift you are born with, it is yours. Embrace her, love her, listen to her, and appreciate her!

Truth 2: You Have Choices

Life is so full of choices. Where there are highs, and there are lows. My extremes have given me the opportunity to feel, not push away or ignore, but instead to step into it, to sit with what is coming up, to feel it, to notice where in the body you feel it, what it feels like, to love it, and that is the gift. They have allowed me to dive deeper into my soul to feel more alive, pure, turned on, tuned in, tapped in, all of it. The divine is ready and wanting to embrace and grace you with all her majesties.

I can choose what I feel. When I let go of fear and judgment, I can fill myself with love. It is as simple as setting the intention with your breath. I breathe in love and exhale all that no longer serves me.

Over the years, I have learned to embrace all of me, especially good stuff. Embracing strengths can be more challenging than accepting weaknesses. So, I set my intentions to catch my negative thoughts and cancel, erase, and rewrite them. Each time I do, I know I am rewiring my brain and empowering myself.

When I think positive, I feel better. Negative thoughts feel so different in my body. What do you want to feel? To find the energy you want, use Intentions, words, your breath, see it, feel it, and make the choice. It takes effort, but wow, once you get there, it is such a gift that you take pride in because you did it, you brought yourself here.

Truth 3: Embracing My Feminine

Let me start with what is masculine vs. feminine. Common feminine traits: intuitive, feeling, nurturing, experiencing, being, collaborative, expressive, creativity, receptive, fluid, allowing, empathetic, sensual, and emotional. Common masculine traits: mind, logical thought, power, decisive action, risk-taking, achieving, controlling, competitive, intellectual, focused, stable, goal oriented, structured, driven, and strong.

I have people that compliment me on being so feminine. I am proud of that because for many years I struggled with my femininity. I preferred hiding my body under baggy clothes. I didn't like my body, and I did everything within my power to change it.

Now I love my body and my life as an empowered woman. I have been told it shows in how I carry myself. So, what does it mean to me to be an authentic feminine woman? These are some of the more common traits that I have embraced:

- Trusting my Intuition
- Allowing myself to fully feel
- Being openly nurturing to myself and others
- Being fully present in every experience

- Working with others through collaboration and supporting other women
- Allowing myself to express my authentic self and my truth
- Connecting with true intimacy with others through empathetic connections
- Expressing my sensual and emotional self

Embracing the feminine aspects of self does not require that you abandon your masculine gifts. Logical thought, expressing external power, being decisive, and taking action can be necessary and appropriate in certain situations. Competition and being focused can serve the empowered woman. It becomes a problem when you can only approach life with these structured, driven, goal-oriented perspectives that begin to drive out your feminine gifts. It goes back to balance; keeping the feminine and masculine in that yin/yang of perfect balance. Knowing when to pull on each is true magic. Knowing this allowed me to start taking better care of myself, loving myself, and loving my body. It all starts within you.

Truth 4: Enjoy the Healing Journey

First, I am divinely perfect. I am not broken; I am transforming. Like a rosebud that opens to a full and beautiful rose, I too am opening to greater wisdom. So, I talk about my healing journey, knowing that it is my transformative journey. I have always been and will always be perfectly imperfect and in a state of opening to my greater self.

"Healing" can look all sorts of ways. It is a journey, a process. It can be instantaneous, or it can take months and years. Each person decides on the length and severity of their journey. Ultimately, we create the journey we are ready for and feel we can handle.

"Healing" can be stimulated by others, such as a therapist, body healer, energy healer, a book, or a class. Each journey is unique and comes in every shape and every form. It always starts with your intentions and your desires to be whole. You control the speed. For me, my journey started with a command to the universe, "Ok, I want to heal from my rape, show me how. Guide me." When I asked, my Tantra classes fell into my lap. For me, Tantra opened major healing channels in my mind and body and was a huge influence on my journey. For you, it may be something else.

There were days where I woke up refreshed and happy and energized, but there were days when I didn't want to get out of bed or be alive. I had to learn to accept both days, and just be kinder, more accepting, and nurturing to myself.

My journey has been messy and hopeful. It has been full of tears and laughter. Sometimes I feel like for every step forward, I take three steps back. Some days I am joyful, others exhausted. My journey is not complete, so I anticipate that I will have days in my future where I will be energized, confused, stagnant, scared, heavy, intense, bored, excited, lonely, and overwhelmed. That is the exciting part. My journey will be filled with all kinds of fun and messy stuff. No matter what, I will grow from it. On those days filled with struggle, my mother always says, "This too shall pass."

Truth 5: Remember to Breathe

Our breath is so important to our journey.

Right now, close your eyes. Put one hand on your heart and the other hand on your belly. Breathe normally for about three to five breaths. You can do it sitting up or laying down, whichever you prefer.

Ok, what did you notice? Did your chest rise? Did your belly rise? If you don't know, do it again and notice. On your normal breaths, what moves more—your belly or chest?

Ideally, you want both to move. We WANT our belly to expand with the breath, we want that breath to fill our lungs and chest and then continue all the way filling your tummy. Take slow deep breaths. If you watch a baby, they know how to breathe properly, just watch one. They take big belly breaths. As we grow older, we seem to get more stressed and less focused, and our breath becomes shorter, and that can have a huge impact on our life and our health.

Prana is a Sanskrit word for breath and for the life-giving force or life force, so that as you inhale, you are receiving life itself, as this equals life energy. Exhaling is letting go, so setting intentions of letting go of that which stops us is a very powerful yet simple exercise.

Breath is something that is free, and you can do it anywhere or anytime. Our bodies are brilliant, they can go days or even weeks without food and/or water, but our body can only go a few minutes without breath. Without breath, we are dead within minutes. Breath is natural, it is pure. I dare you to breathe deep, breathe with intention, and feel your body become freer.

Life is about balance or finding and creating balance. Look at breath... you can only exhale as much air as you took in or inhaled. So as deep as you inhale is only as deep as you can exhale. There is a balance to our breath.

I realized I feel more grounded, alive, and more powerful with deeper breaths. It took me a long time to practice, but now it is effortless. Research says my brain works better, and I can make better decisions when I take deep intentional breaths.

The breath does so many things to your body. It oxygenates your body and organs. Otto Warburg won the 1931 Nobel Prize in Medicine for his work, proving that cancer could not live in an oxygenated state.

The list of benefits of intentional breathing is long. You have better awareness, greater relaxation, improved focus, improved emotional states, decreased stress, lowered blood pressure, boosted immunity, better sleep, reduced food cravings, elevated moods, and expanded states of consciousness. It also facilitates access to higher guidance and clarity, reduces physical pain, and heals wounds, traumas, and grief. Indeed, learning to breathe intentionally is a miracle drug we can all take.

In Conclusion

Remember, you were never broken, you are always whole. Sometimes you may not feel whole, but you are. You have chosen to take a journey of transformation. The messy, unpredictable part is the joy of the journey. Learn to love your journey. This is my TRUTH and I trust it will become yours!

About Stacie Harder

Stacie Harder is a popular speaker, actor, writer, and personal coach. Through her work, she inspires and challenges individuals and groups to find joy in life, by embracing ALL of who you are. She has spent decades perfecting her craft and has mastered the art of successfully integrating and living in balance with the mind, body, and spirit. Schooled at Ball State University, she received advanced training in many areas of personal growth and spiritual arts including Reiki, Tantra Educator, Taoism, and Body Talk. If you desire to awaken to your greatness, clear your blocks, celebrate your sacred sexuality, or dream a bigger life, contact

Stacie at Harderstacie@gmail.com, on Instagram, on her website, or via Facebook.

Website: StacieHarder.com
Facebook: Stacie Harder

14

Contemplations on Oneness and Resistance

By Mira Rubin

All I've ever wanted was to wake up; to be free of the dream that is our separateness from ourselves and from the universe. I had that experience once, of the ineffable—of full and unbounded presence, beyond time and space, beyond personality and belief. For a brief few moments, at the age of 15, I no longer existed as a separate consciousness but became consciousness itself, all-knowing and without story, a pure expression of truth.

Then it was gone, and I was human again, bound to my body, my senses and my history, exiled from that place of peace and perfection. That taste of purity has been both my inspiration and my ruin.

Nothing I've experienced has ever felt so real or so true and I've devoted my life to finding it again. Unable to reconcile transcendence and the mundane, I've often felt like a stranger in a strange land and have been heartbroken to have known such peace and presence only to have had it snatched away.

My deep desire to reclaim that state has inspired a life of spiritual inquiry, a quest to understand the nature of reality and consciousness, and a relentless search for meaning. So, when I was recently told that oneness was the next step on my path to awakening, I chose to dive in to see what I could discover. I wasn't at all prepared for the confusion of thoughts that ensued and the roil of conflicted emotion.

"Is oneness the same as unity?" I asked. The answer was no, so I went to the dictionary for clarification. Unity is defined as a coalescing of multiple parts, while oneness is a unit of one. Unity implies an initial state of separateness, while oneness is whole and singular. By definition, oneness means the absence of separation.

Then I became aware of the terrible irony. The path to enlightenment may be oneness, but the entire human experience is defined by our separateness. Just take a minute to ponder that. No matter how connected we feel, how much love we share, as long as we're having a human experience, we are surrounded by a world that we know by its otherness. We are separate beings, living separate lives, separate from the environment that surrounds us. Our separateness goes so far that we experience ourselves as separate from our bodies, from our emotions and, when we observe them, even separate from our thoughts. It is only in separation that we know our self or know the illusion that we believe ourselves to be.

So, what path is there to oneness when our fundamental experience of ourselves is founded in separation? What if we were to allow the self—that is so rigorously tied to its notions of identity—to dissolve, to disengage from knowing, and to instead connect to being? Perhaps the world would open, and we would become that oneness, seeing and experiencing the whole of the universe as one uninterrupted and complete expression of consciousness.

But how? Oneness is the experience of the moment unadorned by the overlay of belief, judgment, and interpretation. It transcends the boundaries of personality, history, and even time itself, to be an unobstructed expression of universal mind. To achieve an experience of oneness is to transcend the experience of being human, to move into a dimension beyond time and space, a place of pure presence where all and nothing are one and the illusion of separation melts into a boundless and timeless emptiness, void of all distinctions.

In human form, oneness is a paradox, where we have the potential to fluctuate from individuation to universality and back again, the quantum fluctuation between particle and wave, time and no time.

Amidst my musings, a friend reminded me that from the state of presence and perfection, nothing remains that needs to be done in the world. This revelation brought me to entirely unanticipated tears and a rising terror around losing everything I know, losing myself and my identity; a terror around facing a vast void and having no idea whatsoever what life after enlightenment might look like. And then the confusion set in. Awakening has been my heart's deepest desire and yet, despite the blissfulness of the instant that established the trajectory of my life, shockingly, I was overcome by fear when imagining its attainment. I had never really believed the stories about the ego's fight for survival, but here I was experiencing extreme fear of annihilation at the same time I was reaching for bliss.

We are not taught to experience our emotions. We are taught to deny, suppress, and push past them, which drives that emotional energy deeper into our bodies where it crystallizes into physical form if left unattended over time. Allowing myself to be present to the fear and confusion rather than resisting or stifling it has allowed me to move through it while creating an opening and a softening of heart. Gradually, I'm finding a deeper peacefulness and growing sense of presence.

The path to freedom and oneness is presence, and the path to presence is in allowing the experience of what is, without the adornment of projection. But human beings are projection machines. Our experiences become our physiology, with memory triggering thoughts and emotions replete with a matrix of associated chemical, biological, and energetic patterns that crystallize into form.

Resistance to the pure experience of the present moment keeps us locked into the perceptions we assemble to call reality. Our words, ideas, thoughts, identities, and beliefs—are overlays, veneers on the truth of being. All these constructs create the matrix of illusion that keeps us separate from experiencing the unbounded consciousness that we are.

As we expand to include our experiences, as we embrace rather than resist, we open more fully into presence and the we who we know ourselves to be fades to reveal an unencumbered consciousness, a loving and breathing field of possibility. We transcend our humanness, the illusions of good and evil, and the limits of belief. We rise and are freed to become the creative consciousness we are, the boundless, unencumbered creators, both particle and wave rather than fields of crystallized energy.

I'm coming to understand that perhaps oneness is not simply a state at which one arrives in a blinding flash of realization. Perhaps it can also be a process of unfolding—of evolutionary steps into greater awareness and a greater sense of peace. Perhaps awakening can occur over time as a melting of resistance in its myriad forms and a gradual and organic opening of the heart.

About Mira Rubin

A unique mix of social entrepreneur, techie nerd, and coaching genius, Mira Rubin is a visionary following her heart and her calling to create a world that works—while guiding others to manifest their dreams. Trained in NLP, hypnosis, and applied kinesiology, Mira developed a transformational modality in 1987 called Core Connection that she integrates in her work with coaching clients to affect profound, rapid and lasting change. Her clients experience foundational shifts of being that result in expansive new opportunities and accomplishment, an expanded experience of freedom and empowered stewardship of their lives.

An epiphany in November of 2017 set Mira on her mission to save the world and led to the start of the *Sustainability Now* podcast, which shares hope and sustainability tools and practices related to food, energy, housing, waste, water, health, economics, and consciousness—consciousness being key.

Both educator, and artist, Mira spent the 18 years prior to the podcast teaching design and development of interactive, e-Learning, print and web content for her training center, Mira Images, Inc.

During that time, she did technical writing, spoke at multiple professional conferences and authored two highly acclaimed texts.

Website: YourCoreConnection.com
Facebook: @OurSustainabilityNow

15

My Mantra

By Christine Crockett Smith

As part of my current spiritual practice, I have a six-word mantra/meditation that I do every morning. Without fail. Before I get out of bed. Non-negotiable.

Sometimes, if I'm in a hurry for some reason (I always try to allow time so I'm not in a hurry, but some days…) it might just be five minutes of saying each word and sitting with it for a moment.

Other days, I will meditate on each word until it feels complete, and it might take an hour and a half.

But I do it every day. Without fail. It anchors me. It grounds and aligns me. It connects me to the Source of love and joy and peace and grace that then follows me throughout the day.

The first word is **Love.** I believe that there is a force field of love that surrounds each of us and all of us in every moment. I believe it is this field from which we all came and to which we all return when we leave these bodies. It has only good intentions and wishes for us all to have lives filled with joy and purpose and is there to support us in every moment. I open the conduit for this love to flow through me throughout the day, knowing it is limitless and that as I allow the love to flow from me in every interaction, that I am instantly refilled from this limitless Source. Focusing on the word **Love** reminds me to lead with love with every thought, word, and action and to shower it upon others, even without speaking to them, by going forth embodying it and possibly impacting people with just a look or a smile.

The second word is **Light**. This is to remind me to Be the Light as I go about my day. To shine that light in any dark corner I might encounter and to be an example to every person I come into contact with, whether in person, in an email or a text or a phone call—to put forth only positive energy in every interaction. It reminds me to avoid dark conversations, interactions, and energy from others, whether that means ending a conversation, walking away, or not engaging. I believe that in that force field that surrounds each of us and all of us, we get to choose whether we want to use our resources—our time, talent, money, gifts, and energy—to feed its light or its darkness. I choose light. Every moment of every day. Focusing on the word **Light** first thing in the morning reminds me to protect myself with an invisible energy field of Only Love In/Only Love Out. This makes negative energy from others bounce right off so I don't take it on as my own and reminds me to not engage with others who haven't yet discovered their own light.

Faith is the third word and it helps me remember that I've had too many rich, glorious, unexplainable moments and experiences to pretend for even a moment that there isn't a field that exists that I can't see or smell or touch or taste or hear. When I first stepped into my spiritual journey 20 years ago, it was easy to slip back into disbelief when I was surrounded by people who had not had such experiences. I often found myself in a space of doubt, as I didn't have anyone to share my journey with and no one to converse with about it. Am I crazy? Have I lost my mind? Am I reaching for some kind of satisfaction in the ethereal only because I can't find it here? How can I be right when I'm surrounded by so many who think I'm wrong? That's over. I now live in a state of complete acceptance that not only does it exist, it is reaching out to everyone and is grateful when we wake up and listen. My **Faith** is now unshakeable and focusing on that word every morning reminds me to be strong and understanding when met with a doubter; not to take on their doubt.

Trust may seem similar to faith, yet it is different. When I focus on Trust, it is to remind myself that the invisible essence that I have Faith in—whether you call it God, Universal Wisdom, Collective Consciousness, The Field, Source Energy, Angels, Guides, The Universe—has my best interests at heart and if I will simply commit to listening, it will help me find the path of least resistance towards my dharma. I believe that energy is paving my way and pulling together whatever cooperative components are necessary for me to do my work in the world. I know that if

I pay attention, they will help me discover the people, situations, circumstances, and tools to do what I came here to do. Focusing on the word **Trust** every morning lays peace on my heart and diminishes any angst about how my day will unfold. Even if things go some way that I would not have chosen, I am able to look for the lesson immediately. It is always there. I believe we can be 90% happy 90% of the time if we remember to listen and take only inspired action. And even that other 10% is valuable if we can remember to look for and learn the lesson, so that we don't have to learn it again!

Serve is the word that reminds me that I am just a conduit. No thought I have, word I speak, or action I take is mine alone. There are things I am meant to share and when I focus on the word **Serve**, I am asking that the people, circumstances, events, and moments that can benefit from whatever I bring to the table be brought to me and that I will know the best thing to say or do to benefit the situation to its highest good. I believe we are all in this together; that community and human interaction is a significant part of each of our journeys; and that each of us can positively or negatively impact every moment… and that we get to choose. By grounding myself in the word **Serve** every moment, I go forth knowing it is not about me; it is about them. And my job is to recognize the opportunities to use my journey to improve theirs, whoever they are.

My final word may be the most important and the hardest to grasp. It takes a deep understanding of and commitment to the first five to be able to truly embrace and believe in it. The word **Next?** is my invitation to The Divine to show me the best use of my resources in the next moment.

Abraham calls it "segment intending" and it refers to giving ourselves permission to pause between changes as our day progresses. Any time a new person enters a conversation, or we head to a different place or shift to some new activity, we are entering a new segment of that day and of our lives. The opportunities and possibilities are limitless. Taking the time to pause and check in with our Internal Compass can help us make the Next Right Choice. As you get into your car to face traffic; head into a meeting; begin a phone call or write an email or send a text; choose which book to read next… in countless shifts throughout the day, there is guidance waiting to lead us to the Best Possible Outcome if we just remember to check in and ask. When I get off a Skype call, there are never fewer than 100 things on my list that I could do next. By pausing and asking "**Next?**" I know that I will be led to do whatever thing is in the best interest of the most people, and that I will be protected and guided while I do it.

Every morning. Without fail. Before I get out of bed.

About Christine Crockett Smith

Christine Crockett Smith has been on a spiritual journey for over 20 years that has led her to understand that her reason for being here this time around is simply to Raise Consciousness, one interaction at a time. Whether it's working one-on-one, conducting workshops, writing, or speaking to a live audience, her main goal is to help people become more deliberate about the way they live their lives.

Each of us came here to live a life of joy. When our mind, body, spirit, or heart get out of balance, things can go awry, keeping us from living our lives to our fullest potential. If we could each just commit to using our time, talent, money, gifts, and energy to making the world a better place, all of the world's problems and challenges would cease to exist. When we get overwhelmed by listening to all that appears to be going wrong in the world, it can feel as if there is nothing we can do. Feeling out of control can lead to depression and anxiety. By simply deciding to do what we can, with what we have, where we are, we can regain our sense of power as we see how our thoughts, words, and actions can positively impact those around us. Christine's main request of all who seek to leave a positive impact on the world is simple: be intentional. We need your unique blend of energy to help move us along towards our highest potential.

>Website: christinecrockettsmith.com
>Email: christinecrockettsmith@gmail.com

16

What I have created, I have the power to change!

By Debbie Garcia

That which I have created, I have the power to change! That is a powerful statement, one that requires taking full self-responsibility for your life. This journey is about returning to self, to your divine spark of the true essence that you are. The infinite road of gratitude is one that opens up wider and wider as it continues on, allowing one's perception to stretch far and wide beyond what has ever been perceived before.

In this first part of the journey, grab your pen and paper. Let's begin with the very simple tool of the *"I AM"* statement. *I AM* that *I AM* is the most powerful statement that one can use. *I AM* is the name of *divinity*, of *GOD/Source* (fill in whatever label you choose) the infinite wisdom that is this UNI-verse. Begin a list—this is a long list of 100 *I AM* statements and part of your gratitude work.

Take your time; this may take a while. Use the *I AM* meditation by Dr. Wayne Dyer (which you can find by googling online). It is my personal favorite and I like to listen to the music by James Twyman from *The Moses Code*. Use this meditation first and then begin the gratitude homework. Here are examples of the *I AM* to get you started.

I AM grateful because:
- I AM worthy and deserving of greatness.
- I AM enough just the way I AM.
- I AM perfectly healthy with a strong body.
- I AM beautiful and bubbly.
- I AM abundant in all ways.
- I AM shown how to GIVE freely.
- I AM wonderful at giving and receiving LOVE.
- I AM LOVE.
- I AM PURE LIGHT.
- I AM PEACE.
- I AM A ROCKSTAR.
- I AM a courageous warrior.
- I AM grateful for ME.
- I AM grateful for all my experiences, past, present, and future.

These are just *my* examples—use these tools however they feel right for you. There is no way you will mess it up; you cannot screw this up, period. In fact, there is not a right or wrong way to do anything other than how it's right for you. Hey; if this is new for you, I totally get you may not feel it—even as you write it and that is okay. You are perfectly human and remember you don't need to change—you are not broken. It's simply a shift needed of perspectives. I do understand that there are *so many* contributing factors that have laid the course of your life. I am more than compassionate about that life course because mine has given me a keen insight into virtually every type of contrast imaginable. "Without your dark, you wouldn't know your spark," as I say, so take it easy on yourself as we are going to go gently together on this journey back to you—back to self-love and self-appreciation. Now, if you are someone who has done some of this work, or even all of it, then view this as a great refresher practice. Remember, everything happens for divine purpose and this is one of them.

Practice is the key—repeating the new perspective patterns and exercising them within your daily experiences. It's all about your mind and the control of your own thoughts. Impossible to believe at times, but yes, you are the one and the only one who can control what you think or say. The next part of this journey is finding out what you truly want out of life, after we embrace the beauty of our emotional scale. Yes, it's a beautiful discovery not only to be able to feel your emotions and actually understand them but to have to tools to shift any thought and create emotions that work for you, not against you. Yeah, it's your emotions working against you, not the person that you blamed it on. Gratitude glasses will help you see all of this clearly and shine bright lights on new perspectives. Spark the G-vibe moment right there! You Rock!

About Debbie Garcia

"Without your dark, you wouldn't know your spark." I am Debbie Garcia, and my favorite thing in this world to spark the G-vibe (that's the gratitude vibration for you newbies). I am that I am! I am on this planet to bring forward the tools that I've learned along this adventure we call life.

This beautiful, glorious, messy adventure requires a new perspective almost on a daily basis. My favorite part of life is teaching and learning new ways to spark the G-vibe; looking at new ways to improve and move forward in love.

This is for yourself first; which is "Self-First," not selfish, so you can show up for others and be truly who we were put on this earth to be. All of this is based on my opinion, from my experience, and my current perspective, which may change in a nanosecond. What you will find are my personal expressions, opinions, and what's worked for me.

I am opening my practice of gratitude intelligence to the world to teach how to apply it along with emotional intelligence. If what you're doing isn't working, it is safe to consider it may be time to gain a new perspective with the use of some different tools.

It's all in the gratitude moments.

Website: www.angelspeakers.com
Facebook: @Spiritualitygonewild

17

Surrendering to Spirit

By Keleena Malnar and Yeshayah

The will of spirit shall always keep us on a continual path of transformation, yet many times upon our journey we do not listen.

These experiences, at times in a dualistic manner, are to acknowledge the truth of our existence in short periods of time; they are for us to create and know love and to balance ourselves in our existence upon and from Gaia.

This is a story of surrendering to the spirit in times when one believes everything has been perfectly planned in 3D reality yet spirit has another plan or, may we say, a life lesson.

Yeshayah

Feeling exhausted after 30 days of letting go of my past, my home, security, family, and my life as I knew it to be, I settled into my seat on the first of three connecting planes to my final destination, where spirit had asked me to go.

My flight from Amsterdam took me to my first connection—Iceland. At the Icelandic airport, I stopped at one of the local restaurants where I had my first encounter on this journey of spirit, speaking to me through a woman, but I did not listen.

It was a serve-yourself buffet. In line, there was a woman dishing herself up her own meal. She leaned in and whispered to me, "Take more food and fill your plate because it is very expensive." My reaction, my thought, was that I did not need very much food; therefore, I did not fill my plate and I felt a resistance to listening to this woman. I doubted myself and because of my exhaustion, I was not in line with spirit, yet spirit was guiding me through this woman and I did not listen. I proceeded to the checkout where the woman rang up my meal. I was shocked at the amount it was costing me considering the amount I had on my plate.

After finishing my delicious meal and wishing I had taken more, I realized spirit had spoken to me through this woman who had advised me to take more, but ego thought it knew better. All I could think was darn it; I already missed a message from spirit!

After finishing my meal, I realized that my carry-on bag was not by my side. I hurried back to where the woman told me to take more food. There was a security officer standing and guarding my bag until the rightful owner returned for it. Here I realized that in this situation, spirit was also protecting me and my important personal belongings. I do not have much anymore, as I had trusted in spirit and given almost all of my personal belongings away before this trip. It surprised me that there was a security man watching over my carry-on bag. It was as if the angels had sent him, and I realized, through my tiredness and exhaustion, that I was safe.

Keleena

It had been quite a day, running in the early morning hours to gather some of Yeshayah's favorite things to make him feel at home, and to get the house ready for him, as well as to undertake my regular daily activities. I was feeling his exhaustion, yet I was so excited that Yeshayah was on his way to me. I knew it was going to be a long tiring trip for him. We had planned that at each connecting airport we would have the chance to speak.

Our first attempt at connecting while he was in Iceland did not go as anticipated and his layover time was very limited. The network connection was quite poor and limited our conversation to numerous attempts at non-connected and dropped phone calls and messages that were not going through. Frustrated, I surrendered; everything will not always go as we plan it and we must surrender to what spirit has divinely planned for us.

Anticipating some kind of connection, a message finally came through from Yeshayah to say that he was boarding his four-hour flight to Boston. I felt that once in the United States, our connection would be better and that we would have plenty of time to talk, as it was a three-hour layover until his final connection to me. I kept thinking how we had been so excited to finally be back together after these 30 days apart. But it was also a very emotional time period for him, as he had unselfishly been releasing all that he knew to be together here with me, to see what our spiritual journey had in store for us. I awaited his phone call from Boston.

Yeshayah

The plane trip from Iceland to Boston went smoothly. As I approached security and the homeland security officer, he asked me when I was going home. I said I do not know; I am visiting my girlfriend but that was not enough to let me through. They took me to an interrogation room to ask me questions. I wanted to message Keleena to tell her what was happening; however, I was told I could not use my phone. My thought was that I was not allowed to use it for phone calls. I tried to message, then it was explained to me that I needed to put my phone away.

I was sitting in a room and I thought to myself, this is just like a movie. I had not done anything wrong but they called my name. They began grilling me with questions that I answered from my highest truth. The same questions were asked repeatedly about why I was here, about the details of my personal relationship with Keleena, what I did back home for work, and so on. After three different officers inquired about my personal life and the work that I would be doing with Keleena, the first officer asked about my jewelry. One was the Vesica Pisces necklace that Keleena and I had both acquired while in Glastonbury, England. The other was my Shiva necklace. I explained the meaning behind both. I felt that after explaining that the necklace depicted Shiva dancing on the demon of ignorance, he had a realization. I then thought back to a moment in time when I had walked through a city back home and a man had approached me and said, "It is time for you to start dancing." This is now what I am here to do in my work with Keleena in the States, and in that exact moment this was what I was doing with this police officer.

My work is to awaken others from their ignorance. I explained to the officer that the Vesica Pisces shows God and Goddess as two circles combined, creating a center shape representing the third eye of intuition and knowledge. This represents a sacred marriage and the eye of the Vesica Pisces represents the light.

I also explained how Keleena and I were participating in an event for sacred partnerships and that the Vesica Pisces represented this. I explained to him how the love we have for one another is the light we radiate as we tell our lifelong coming-together story and conduct our healing and activation work. Our finding one another has given hope to others on this same journey; that the person that we have known all our life was coming will appear if we continue to follow the signs and synchronicities that spirit gives us. It relays the message that true unconditional love exists. I noticed that the officer became nervous and he then apologized for asking me so many questions. After all of this, the officer told me to go home before the 90 days were up, not to get married, and to obtain the correct visa. They let me go. At this point, I did not know it had been two hours. I walked out the door and immediately messaged Keleena. I knew she would be worried because there was no communication from me.

Keleena

When Yeshayah landed in Boston, I was elated he was in the USA as he messaged his arrival. He had told me he was in line for security and that the line was really long. Everything was going well and then it was as if his phone turned off. Communication ceased, and I knew at this point that I needed to tune in to higher wisdom. My intuition was that he was pulled over for questioning and I knew I needed to keep my vibration up and keep my own thoughts positive. I was quite worried after the first hour went by, then it went just over the second hour. I knew and trusted that if anything were to happen it would be in the hands of the divine.

When Yeshayah finally came back online, he was frustrated running through to the next checkpoint security. He had less than an hour to get to his gate on the other side of the airport. On my end, the driver I had hired to drive me and to pick him up from this late-night arrival was confirming the time to get me for the hour's drive to the airport. At this point, I wondered if he would make his flight as I knew it was boarding but said nothing, as I did not want to worry him. I held off the driver, asking him to wait until he heard from me.

I felt Yeshayah's frustration, exhaustion, and his hunger. I asked the angels to, "Please help with the situation and allow everything to go as need be for where we are to be in the moment right now." Tired and hungry myself, I began to doubt he would make his flight as he had not been through security and his flight was leaving in 30 minutes.

Yeshayah

Now, I was at the security checkpoint and the officers were chatting, taking their time and having a good time, while I was in a hurry. Everything was in the boxes to go through and then they pulled my carry-on. In frustration and exhaustion, I had not known that I needed to take my laptop out, as they had not told me; it was my first time doing this. I then had to repeat going through security with my laptop out. This time they saw my external hard drive was also in my bag. I now had to go through for the third time. I was completely frustrated.

After this long delay, I ran as fast as I could to the gate that was scheduled. When I got there, I asked if the plane had left and they said no. I was happy it was not boarding yet, even though it was past the time of take-off. I told Keleena I had made it! Then I noticed it was not the right plane for my destination. The plane gate had moved to another location. When I got to the correct gate the plane had already left. I was frustrated yet accepted that all of this had happened. It did not make sense to me.

I spoke with Keleena and she told me there is a reason I needed to be in Boston overnight, as her last flight home went through Boston and her plane was canceled. Spirit had led her to some spiritual work she needed to do here and felt that I, as the masculine, was there to complete my part of the work—to balance the love in this area. Keleena reminded me to connect with the Lady Nada Temple that resides over Boston in the etheric realm, as she did while she was there. As she said this, I felt the energy come into my body.

Keleena had set up a hotel for me for the night and the next morning I felt the presence of Lady Nada strongly within me. My hotel bill total was in synchronicity with the number of the Ascended Masters and holy trinity—333. This was our divine sign that all is well and that we have to trust in all that happens.

Keleena

At 11 in the evening, Yeshayah called me back to say that he had missed his plane. I immediately canceled the car, and had emails sent out to my clients for the next day, as the rescheduled flight was now landing during my client session times. I am very grateful that the clients were very understanding about what had happened, and the driver was able to accommodate the next day. This incident did not affect one person; it affected many over a three-day period. All plans had changed for us, my clients, and my family.

This all led me to see that time exists in this third-dimensional earth reality, yet those of us doing the higher work of spirit must stay in our sacred, loving hearts surrendering, trusting, and allowing all—for what spirit is guiding us to do. We may not understand at first, but when we truly stay aligned it is easily accepted and the work is completed.

Our trust in our higher selves and spirit is quite important on this journey as everything is divinely timed. We may believe that we have everything perfectly planned at any given moment until spirit clearly shows us the way. Our work is to listen, follow our hearts, and have trust that all is well. When we feel that all is well, all will be well. This is the law of attraction in action.

And so, it is.

In Divine Love & Grace,

Keleena & Yeshayah

About Keleena Malnar

Keleena's purpose as a Wayshower and spiritual teacher in service is to teach and guide humanity through their ascension process. Speaking all of the Universal Light Languages (the language of love), Keleena is a key code activator here to activate all souls through their DNA at a cellular level, collectively or privately for each individual's specific needs.

As a Wayshower for ascension, she helps move you from the conditioned ego to the sacred heart to merge with the sacred masculine mind in divine union activating your sacred voice.

She guides you to live passionately as your authentic self, from your Sacred Heart, in your highest truth, wisdom, and grace.

Keleena helps elicit clients' natural healing abilities for physical, mental, emotional, spiritual, and physiological healing. Her guides have given her the title of a Multidimensional Quantum Energy Healer and refer to her as "One who knows the Power of the Heart."

As a High Priestess of Isis, she is an initiator and activator of the Sisters of the Rose of the Order of the Magdalene. Her healing modalities and abilities have all come through her embodiment of who she has been in past lives. She conducts what she refers to as Isis healing.

Her collective work is to assist all of God's children in their ascension process by moving them from their deepest fears into love.

Some of her other abilities are as a Trance Medium Channeler with the gift of all six senses. She is also a Reiki Master & Teacher, Shamanic sound healer through light language vibrations in vocalization, a psychic, a clear, pure conduit and channel for Source and feels her abilities are unlimited. She conducts workshops and retreats on ascension, sacred heart, and light language. She is also a spiritual intuitive energy artist, a writer of divine guidance, poetry, prose, and inspirational quotes, and loves spiritual photography.

Keleena has vowed to use her gifts in the highest honor, love, and light for all from her pure heart. Her greatest desire is to see all people collectively stand in unity, love, compassion, and in the Oneness that we all are.

Website: Keleenamalnar.com

Facebook: @Keleena Malnar

About Yeshayah

Yeshayah received a vision at a very early age of three years old. This vision was a fortress where people came together during a chaotic period. After this period ended, the people in the fortress who survived worked together to restore Mother Earth to her paradise state.

At 17, Yeshayah had a more profound awakening with the power of thought and started creating. Yet with this, karma also set in for his journey of clearing for his ascension.

In 2003, at only 25, he built a spiritual center in the Netherlands where he taught divine yoga and conducted meditations and other spiritual practices. During 2005 at his center, Yeshayah created a large-scaled third-dimensional cube of Metatron to activate his own Merkaba and that of others. This was part of his vision of the fortress coming to life.

When Yeshayah started speaking Light Language in 2005, he began utilizing it to activate clients and other people to bring them into a higher state of consciousness.

Yeshayah has been guided by Lady Nada his entire life and knew that in this life, it was about finding true unconditional love. He learned of the twin-flame path and experienced these findings in his own life. He has been led to his Sacred Partner or twin flame, Keleena, in this twin-flame journey.

Yeshayah is a Quantum Energy Healer, Light Language Activator, and Melchizedek initiator/activator for souls to receive more love light from source for their ascension process. He is also a Divine Yoga Instructor and has studied several martial arts throughout his lifetime. Through his healings, he restores the connection to source through the heart of creation in faith.

Together, Yeshayah assists Keleena in Unity with Sisters & Brothers of Light workshops as she teaches, initiates and activates the Magdalene Sisters of the Rose, while he conducts the Melchizedek ascension path.

Yeshayah believes when one knows thyself, thy will be done.

Website: https://www.williammelchizedek.com/
Facebook: william.melchizedek

KELEENA MALNAR AND YESHAYAH

18

Steps of Healing from Abuse

By Monica Augustine

I was recently a speaker on the "Enlightened Women ~ Enlightened You Summit" organized and led by Dr. Ruth Anderson. Ruth asked me to write up my "Steps of The Healing Process." In my case, it was the healing journey from mental, physical, and sexual abuse. Your healing journey may be of a different nature. These steps will help with any healing process.

I am going to start from the beginning. If you feel you are farther along than the beginning, please pick up where you feel you are at this time and please email me if you'd like support at energiahealingarts@gmail.com

Reclaiming your life, self-worth, and self-love

Acknowledgment

Practice greeting every uncomfortable feeling or emotion as a message asking to be heard and seen. This requires taking a break from busyness. It's important to make time for this. If you hear or feel an inner tug to pay attention, and you don't have time in that moment, you will need to tell the part of you that is speaking up that you will make time at such an such a time (be specific with your time). Sit down and tune in to him or her. Be specific and make the time to help.

Acknowledge the message that needs to speak. Say, "I hear you. I'm listening," like you would talk to a young child. Acknowledge this pain and hurt with compassion and care. Don't dismiss it, push it down, or try to get rid of it. It will come out in some way or form. Sometimes, I will even say to this hurt part that is speaking, "I'm sorry that happened and that is not OK. I will keep you safe now."

Morning is a good time to check in with these inner messages, even if it is for just a few minutes. A good question to ask at this time is, "What is the gift/silver lining/message in this uncomfortable feeling or thought?"

Acceptance

It's important to accept all the emotions related to what you've been through, yes, even the one most everyone cringes at—anger. Anger is a natural response to feeling violated. It is a valuable emotion that helps you set boundaries. When expressed mindfully, with the intent to protect and not to harm, it gives you the energy and firmness to set boundaries in situations where they were crossed and violated, such as an abusive experience. Anger says, "Hey, hear me. I was hurt. I am going to take care of myself and stand up for myself now that I am older and I can!"

Helpful tip: Sometimes I will say out loud, "I'm feeling angry." I just note it and it helps me to move along. I try not to say, "I am angry," because my practice is to understand that I am not my feelings. I have feelings, but they do not define me. I can choose how I relate to them. I can use their energy and information to give me insight and help me take action.

Accept that this journey of healing may be layered, like the layers of an onion. Practice accepting you, and your journey, free of comparison. How? In the moment, notice you are being hard on yourself, breathe, tune in, and feel the energy of your feet on the ground. Then, feel the energy in your heart area/chakra. Just feel. Sense your essence. Sense your unique perspective and value. Honor who you are and what you've been through.

Observation

Cultivate a practice of observation. Practice observing your thoughts and feelings without believing in, responding to, or identifying with them. It's as if you are watching a film of your thoughts, feelings, and experiences. Use this technique, especially when you feel triggered. Pause. Breathe. Observe. If you find you are caught up in your feelings, thoughts… It's OK… we all do it. Just reset… with self-compassion.

Developing a daily meditation practice is a way I cultivated this skill of observing. If you'd like some guided meditations, send me an email through my website: http://www.energia-transformyourlife.com

Building

Begin to build your confidence, self-esteem, and self-worth. Here are some ways I did this as a young person: I learned piano, guitar, singing, songwriting, gymnastics, painting... pick one thing you like and grow your skill, competence, and confidence. Confidence in one thing tends to carry over into others. When you see yourself developing and creating a beautiful skill, you begin to build self-esteem, joy, and self-worth. The positive vibration in this activity begins to attract more experiences like it.

Question

Begin to question negativity in your own mind and in others you relate to. Ask, "What purpose is served by looking at things or myself in this negative way?" Then, choose which thoughts you focus on and which ones you let go.

Courage

Practice strengthening the courage to say "YES" to something different than you have in the past. For example, I practice saying "YES" to having kind friends, support, abundance, a gift, and new thoughts. Practice saying new affirming thoughts to yourself. For example, "I actually like the way I sound, look, think, care for others... "

Failing

When you feel like you are going backwards in your healing process, reset yourself with compassion. Try to avoid punishing yourself. It's OK. Noticing what you are doing is a positive step. When you notice old thoughts, feelings, and behaviors, pause. These are just old habits, nothing more. Use this as a moment to reset and move forward.

Accept Support and Happiness

Strengthen your communication with your higher self, God, your faith, Angels, and all forms of support. Strengthen the knowledge of how important you are to the whole. You matter. Ask for what you want and need. Acknowledge receiving by saying, "Thank you."

Personally, I am learning to be comfortable feeling happy. If you can learn to get used to pain and hurt, you can learn to get used to accepting joy, abundance, and the life you envision for you, your family, and those around you. It's your choice and your responsibility to take care of you. If you are not experiencing life the way you'd like in any area, ask yourself, "Do I feel unworthy of what I desire?" "Do I feel guilty for desiring this experience?" Listen to your answer without judgement and as an observer. Notice what your answer is. If it is "No," continue inquiring... then ask yourself, "What is my block? What am I learning?" I also pray for help seeing what I am not seeing. This is a very helpful way to have blocks removed. Try not to have a way you think the answer should come, or you may not see it ☺.

Welcome having what you need and desire.

Compassion and Forgiveness

Every person is different. We each have different personalities, needs, and coping strategies.

Everyone's personality takes in the same information and processes it differently. So, it's important to have compassion for your healing journey without comparing it to others and to have compassion for theirs without judging it by yours.

Ultimately, we need to cultivate compassion for ourselves and for the person or people who were abusive. That doesn't mean you say, "It's OK, I know you didn't mean it." It means, "I wish you a peaceful and joyful life, but this is not OK and I don't allow people to treat me this way. You need to seek help for this behavior and I will not allow you to abuse me or anyone else in our home while you figure that out."

One of the challenging areas early in the healing journey is forgiving yourself. When we are young and we have been abused, we learn dysfunctional ways of thinking about ourselves. We lose trust in people and doubt ourselves. We tend to think that what happened was our fault. In my case, I was told that what they did to me was my fault. They told me I had asked for it.

As I began to remember that I was sexually abused, which I had suppressed until I was about 24, I noticed habits such as feeling responsible for making men happy, for pleasing them and making them feel better. I was sometimes promiscuous and began to wonder why I was like that and why men of all ages seemed to know I was broken in that way and approach me. It's like a part of my brain was on autopilot when it came to men. They, most likely, were also hurt in some way.

I also had a strong belief that my looks were what made me valuable. So, I put a lot of effort into keeping that up, because I wanted to be valued and loved.

It takes courage to acknowledge these things and to try to change how you think and feel. You just think that's the way you are. I remember a moment when I was 24, when I began to remember what happened and decided I wanted things to change. I began a new relationship with a man (whom I later married) who was nothing like what I'd grown up with, and I began to take steps to change inside. I sought counseling, continued prayer for healing and began to meditate.

It wasn't easy. Old habits die hard, especially ones that are so deeply ingrained with strong negative feelings. I failed and fell several times. At those moments, I wondered, "How am I ever going to forgive myself? I hate that I feel this way! I hate that I have these beliefs!"

It's been a long road, but I have learned to treat myself the way I imagine God would treat me or see myself as my husband sees me—through the eyes of love.

After self-compassion and forgiveness, the next step is compassion and forgiveness for the person(s) who treated you badly. Harboring hate and anger is an understandable response. It's important to acknowledge and accept these feelings first. However, if you want to be free, you've got to take the next step and forgive.

This can begin by seeing that the person who hurt you was unconscious and hurting themselves. If they weren't, there is no way they could undertake those hurtful actions.

Somewhere along the line of their lives, they were hurt and made to feel bad about themselves. When I consider this, I can let go of feeling only anger and hatred for them. I see them in a new light of compassion.

Forgiveness is a next step. When I forgive, I free myself from being tied to and defined by what happened to me. When I forgive those who hurt me, I put the past behind me and walk into a new future. I stop being defined by the pain of my past.

Meditation practice

I have been meditating now for about 25 years. Meditation helped me get off antidepressants and see that I am separate from my thoughts and beliefs—and that they aren't all true. This was a huge revelation to me—to observe my thoughts without thinking they are all true. I can choose the thoughts that are helpful and let go of the rest.

Many times, it was challenging to meditate because lots of uncomfortable feelings would surface. Part of meditating is letting them arise without giving them energy, without focusing on them, just acknowledging them and letting them go. Sometimes, I found myself crying, feeling angry, or sad. Over time, I learned to trust that feelings come and go and everything is OK. I am safe now. I can feel things without having them overwhelm me. Whenever these feelings come up, I acknowledge them, let them go, and return to my breath.

I've learned to see the breath as the gift of life, a gift from God. I've grown my trust in Divine Life and Love. God is Good, not a punisher, as I was brought up to believe. I am learning to trust God's plan for me. Meditation has helped me to recognize and let go of limiting beliefs and embrace a new way of being, one of acceptance and inclusion.

If you haven't meditated before, I would recommend starting with about 5-10 minutes, once or twice a day. First thing in the morning is a good time, because it helps you start the day with a calm, clear mind. After all these years, meditation is something I look forward to every morning.

I hope these steps are helpful to you in your own healing journey. If you have any questions or would like some support, you can reach me at:

www.energia-transformyourlife.com

My quiet time with God

Love, life, my heart, soul, spirit guides, however you want to say it is welcome…

I began a habit that I do every day, no matter how busy or how important everything I need to do seems…

I sit, listen, feel gratitude for this life, the people in it, the earth, nature… cultivating that connection feels like nourishment and like heaven on earth.

You can do it. You can live the life you feel is possible in your heart. That feeling is not placed there by accident. I believe our deepest and purest desires are God's/love's desires for us as well.

With Love,
Monica

About Monica Augustine

My career passion is to support clients to gain clear insight, release inner blocks, and heal, so they can take positive action to experience the life they desire. I gain information by asking questions, actively listening, and using my empathic, clairaudient, and clairvoyant skills. I then use Reiki to release and clear inner blocks and Life Coaching to support positive action steps. I have training as an Intuitive Reader and am certified as a Reiki Master Teacher and Life Coach.

In addition, I founded and directed Wildflower School of Voice in Boulder, CO, for 20 years before selling it at the end of 2014 to transition into my new work full-time.

On the personal side, I have lived in Colorado for 29 years, have been married to my husband Kevin for 24 years, and have two boys, Greg and Will. I love to be with my family, sing, exercise, and devote time to friends and my spiritual practice.

Website: energia-transformyourlife.com

19

Readings From our Enlightened Angels

By Sheryl Glick

It was a pleasant surprise to hear from Dr. Ruth Anderson, a former guest on my internet podcast show *Healing From Within*, who at that time discussed her book, *One Love: Divine Healing at Open Clinic* and our continuing spiritual observations and practices as spiritual women walking our path. It seems we are often placed in our everyday lives with many souls who have little awareness of their true nature and as such, we are always working to help so many people awaken to the true magnificent potential of their inner soul wisdom. It is lovely to be in touch and in tune with individuals such as Ruth who are in alignment to their guides and to their life destiny as soul healers and messengers on the planet purposely to bring hope to our tired, troubled nation and our world during these very challenging days. As soon as Ruth shared with me that Archangel Michael had let her know that 500,000 angels or light beings are present on the earth now to assist humanity move to a higher level of consciousness and awareness, I began to meditate and tap into their energy to try to discover if there were ways I and others might begin to assist in this auspicious task.

Archangel Michael is a guide who I believe has been working with me and so many others over the past 25 years, perhaps before I was even unaware of it. I have always been trying to understand the human condition and the emotions of fear and love that permeate all life experiences. Now I finally know what I always knew deep within, even in childhood, that we were souls having a physical life for the purpose of remembering who we are and always have been: soul beings of eternal creative life force energy. Through the challenges of a physical life we begin to remember "All that is" with joy and gratitude as each experience we are given offers opportunities to refine our heart energy for greater compassion and love.

In meditation today, I let the angels know Ruth had contacted me and asked how we may help with their mission of hope and love at this time. This is the vision they showed me.

Readings from our Enlightened Angels
April 11, 2019

I saw the Angels taking the children's hands and our hands, as we are like children to them and they guide us to stand tall and walk to the Light with smiles and slow quiet energy. In other words, not rushing or being embroiled in chaos.

I felt cobwebs being cleared from old structures and ideas, places, and our eyes to reveal the truth or transparency needed.

The Mighty Warriors extend their beautiful powerful wings, uncloak their robes or capes, and join the ordinary ranks of people as they stand next to them to help open their third eye and visual connection to Spirit and increase awareness for their personal power, opening hearts and minds to acceptance and feelings.

They ride on white horses across meadows and worlds rapidly and like the wind.

"Just raise your arms like the wings of birds that stack up one on top of another.

Reaching to the sun and heights of love with prayer, song, and peaceful engagement in groups, families, and workplaces.

Make it all happier and filled with joy

BUILD and reach higher… A little more each day

We are the support next to each of you, bringing a better awareness of possibilities now and for the future."

April 12, 2019

"Like the Lone Ranger rearing up on his white horse and serving the people; fighting the corruption of his time in an honest way

And like Batman who wore a mask at times

Two identities: One for everyday life and one for Justice behind the scenes.

Man of La Mancha, just an old man on a quest to honor all and do good.

He protected Dulcinea the bar maiden in the tavern.

A righteous quest for the dignity of all

No judgment, just fearlessness

Action against the unjust

Heroes who risk all for Truth and Righteousness

It is still the quest of Spirit to aid humanity in its search for goodness.

We come to pull those who can connect to us in dreams or meditation
And bask in the healing energies of eternal life

In dreams and visits and vision we connect in the energy of color: of red and orange light. (The first two chakras of the physical world and personal relationships.)

Feel the freshness of air and breathe in the newness of spring as the accordion or fan of light opens and renews Man and World with hope and beauty.

The littlest creatures beloved by children and cared for are how WE love humanity and each living thing no matter how small or seemingly inconsequential.

That is not so—each particle of life is important to the Web of Consciousness.

Like an unbroken horse never ridden before, it tries to knock the rider off but eventually knows they are safe and allows us to attach with the rider and be as one.

They give up the fight and continue the task."

April 17, 2019

"We rest and land in gentleness on the earth. The pain we feel is immense.

We hold you as the Moon cradles the light of the sun and an adult cradles a child in quiet peaceful love.

For the moment the sword is surrendered and it is a time for silent respect to reign in the hearts of those we attend to.

We heal those at their solar plexus chakra, instilling hope, confidence, and respect for their spiritual goals and their connection to each other.

Many who cannot balance their energetic forces will return to Spirit.

Like as on a see-saw ride will catapult strongly and quickly up

Healing now comes from giving up the pain and reality of physical life

And being trusting—free—able to rest in peace

As we connect to you and you to each other

<u>*The chain of Hope and Peace will burn bright.*</u>

Just allow us to be with you at all times: Night and Day

Ask for us to enter and share the best of Heaven now with Earth

Like Star Bursts, love spreads and warms the planet and hearts."

April 30, 2019
"A march across the valley through mountains

Side by side, row after row, endless power and discipline to walk the world as the Jewish people walked through the Red Sea and desert to find God

WE will help you triumph in light and be FREE.

WE begin with the children and lift them up to hold their own sense of goodness and help the elders be more aligned to their own innocence

We will fan and cool the rage and anger with Miracles

Like the boy who lives after being thrown down three flights in a mall in Minnesota

And the Rabbi who with love blesses the woman who gave her life to save him so he could speak the truth to his congregation and to the nation that the President of the United States gave his time, effort, and blessings to help the Jewish people and to end hatred and return us to PEACE

The women and angels, like lifting a tree from a sprout to a giant timber, will encourage nurturing Women's Rights and nature to provide the best of their life force so the planet can stand married to life, love, and new beginnings.
The PAIN of relationship will be given up for more interactive processes and we will insist on equality for Men and Women, Black and White, Jewish, Christian, or Islam

WE will insist on allowing groups to meet and find common ground

It is not a request, but a Divine Decree!"

August 1, 2019
"Like the Tree of Life

A giant evergreen: each branch supporting the next tier of life.

Shelters all life… the birds sit on the branches, humans sit under the shade of the branches.

All benefit when the tree is strong and healthy

But people snip away at the overgrowth, and the excess but, like a Bonsai tree sculptured and shaped by creative intention, it is still beautiful and healthy

Spirit is helping humanity at this time to prune the waste and reveal the interconnectedness of all life

Some may have been crippled by the illusions of the world and societal thinking

Time to know… to feel… to acknowledge the blessings of Spirit's love and stand united in the beauty and goodness of physical life as it relates to the real treasure, which is being part of Divine Love and Expansion.

Trust! You will find your way forward
Fears will be eliminated

New Life will emerge."

If we look at these messages and others coming through to many mediums and visionaries at this time of complete upheaval throughout the world: cataclysmic weather changes, shortages in food production, and clean water supplies, wars, disease, political, economic, and social division, we see that the time to come together and unite for the good of all can only be accomplished if we truly know who we are as spiritual beings having a physical life for that revelation is the key to ending fear, division, injustice, and to support healing.

Many years ago, after a series of mystical experiences that I could not explain with my logical mind, I found myself experiencing feelings within that related to a life that was more than my physical experience. As I began to quiet my mind I began to know my inner thoughts in a way that went beyond the five senses and the way I was used to experiencing the physical world. I became aware that I was able to use an intuitive sense that had nothing to do with my mind, years of education, or life experiences. It was a sense of knowingness and awareness of history, our humanity, and the past in a way that went beyond normal explanation. In dreams and in my interactions with numerous people—that I later discovered were Spiritual guides brought into my conscious reality for the important purpose of realizing my life plan and my inner soul being—a new awareness emerged, enabling me to constantly review past beliefs seen purely from a physical indoctrination into this time, place, and present life experience to another way. I am incredibly more able to accept new ways of knowing myself and those who walk this journey with me, and to discern the true meaning of life.

How thankful I am for the opportunity to experience life, having my feet in two worlds—the physical and the spiritual. How much better life becomes when we are awakened to the true possibilities of our dynamic and ever-changing, eternal, soul being.

Whether in a body or in pure energy, the soul is the essence and complete oneness of Spirit's Intelligence and Universal Love, and travels with us through time and space, lifetime after lifetime, as we gather experiences to refine our already magnificent soul. Death, in my observation, is the next destination or adventure on our continuous circle of life.

There really then is no death, only the unfolding of the infinite layers of realities that exist within us, both here in this world, and beyond. These layers are filled with the excitement and wonderment of the beauty of nature, friendship, memories, and experiences gathered during many lifetimes. We must know that energy cannot be destroyed, so the energy of our thoughts and heart impulses must return to the place most people think of as Heaven, but is really simply the evolving expansion of creative life energy that is eternal. Whether in life, or whether in Heaven, we are continually growing in our ability to gather love, compassion, and to conquer any negativity or fear that might reside in our energy.

As a hospice volunteer, I have been privileged to serve end-of-life patients and their families by providing any assistance to make their transition to their new life as gentle and free of pain and fear as is humanly possible. Sometimes

I was only meant to hold a person's hand, or listen to remembrances from their life stories, or to hand them a glass of water. Whatever interaction ensued, I tried to instill great trust in the final act of transcendence, knowing all was well and would be well as they journeyed beyond their physical body. None of us are ever alone, as we are surrounded by loved ones in Spirit, from the beginning of our life to the end, so know therefore, death is just a new beginning.

I had joined hospice partially to help those crossing over and also their families to see that death was not a punishment, as many people left behind often believed. Many people want their loved ones to live forever in this physical world; however, this is not possible or desirable. Death for so many individuals is viewed as final and is sometimes conceived of as a deep plunge into the unknown darkness and seemingly nothingness, especially for those who have no belief in an afterlife. Concluding that being away from life and physical pleasures of the world is a punishment, for many people, no matter the age of the person, or the reason for their loved one's passing, death may be approached with overwhelming fear. However, death as a punishment is perceived that way only by the living. Those that have crossed over know the truth that they are whole, free, and very much alive.

In reading my next book *New Life Awaits*, I know you will discover much synchronicity with your own daily observations. You will find comfort in validating many of your dearest wishes for living life with an expansive and bolder approach, creating new perspectives and new thoughts. These will take you in the direction that your souls and hearts were born to experience. You will be unencumbered by the rules and limitations of the societal or family systems that have temporarily made you forget that you are an amazing loving, magnificent entity born to walk in delight on our beautiful landscape and in spiritual light. When new life awaits you, always know you do not walk alone.

Each of us, I have discovered, have a specific unique destiny, experiences, and challenges that are included in a life plan or itinerary that comes into this world with us at conception. At conception the soul part of life merges with physical body for the ultimate purpose of exploring our divine potential. I was reminded only recently that true happiness can only be found by understanding our true worth as divine beings having a physical life. When we are able to discern our part in the process of creating happiness for ourselves and others, we will also recognize that the instinctual need to grow and put forth our presence in the world is really our reason for being.

As spiritual beings having a human life experience, readers will also take away with them a greater awareness of human life because in these tumultuous, changing modern times we must be allowed to develop a more heightened and astute social consciousness. This is in order to bring about worldwide cooperation in dealing with health, educational, medical, and political concerns affecting all of life. It is also to bring about evolution in all our communities, spiritually and physically, offering much needed new ways to go about eliminating injustice, the proliferation of crime, conquering disease, reinventing social graces, and finding a way to integrate higher Universal Laws for wellbeing and success into our human daily lives. If we are being watched from above by those who live in gentler conditions than here on Earth and who with love and hope for our advancement as a human species expect us to expand and create more loving interactions and conquer warring impulses, the choice to do this is non-negotiable.

It is a big job to awaken and realize your true potential as a divine force for change and improvement personally and collectively, but it is also amazing to learn the truth. I hope within your heart you will find a new beginning for your own evolution.

About Sheryl Glick

Sheryl Glick, a New York-based accredited Reiki energy healer/medium, offers individual and group sessions and teaches healing and spiritual development. Sheryl taught in New York City schools and holds a BA and MS in Education/Literature. She is a member of the International Association of Reiki Professionals and a longtime hospice volunteer.

She is the author of *Life Is No Coincidence: The Life and Afterlife Connection* and *The Living Spirit: Answers for Healing and Infinite Love, Sharing Stories of Spiritual Communication, Healing Energies, and Miracles.* She is currently completing the third book in the trilogy; *New Life Awaits: The Eyes of Spirit Share Evolution Revolution Global Awakening.*

Sheryl Glick is the host of *Healing from Within,* an internet radio show heard on her website, www.sherylglick.com, www.dreamvisions7radio.com and www.webtalkradio.net which includes over 700 interviews that explore the many facets of universal energy healing and the aligning of our physical and inner being for a complete, healthy, and dynamic human experience. Sheryl has worked with prominent speakers and visionaries worldwide who are seeking to help humanity awaken to greater self-awareness of their inner eternal soul being.

Sheryl opens her mind and heart to help others attain a higher view of life through shared coincidences, synchronistic happenings, and miracles and connect to Spirit's for the improvement of humanity.

Website: sherylglick.com
Website: webtalkradio.net

20

Grandma's Infinite Healing Blessings

By Sommer Joy Ramer

I have experienced a tremendous amount of resistance to writing this and equally feel it has been a breakthrough opportunity for me as well.

I knew the invitation from Ruth was important and was direct guidance from the angels. I just did not know how challenging the week following September 24, 2019 would turn out to be.

This particular week became a sudden, grief-saturated and deeply insightful week. I have witnessed a deep unraveling, breakthrough, and coming full circle journey.

This specific timeframe became a significant mess of golden nuggets revisiting me from my past. On that Tuesday, it hit me like a freight train.

The reminder of that tragic day eight years ago, my dearest friend and beloved Grandma had died.

On Tuesday, September 24th, 2019, I had gotten up early, finding myself showing up for life by engaging in the brutal discipline of waking up at 7:AM. That was two hours earlier than normal for me. I then meditated for 1 hour and 11 minutes. This purifying morning routine has been changing my life and turning up the volume when it comes to my relationship to spirit. I was so proud of myself!

After the meditation, I opened my eyes to a vibrationally heightened reality, looking over the soft-current waters of the beach I live on. The first thing I saw was a pod of magical dolphins, who are always a sign of a visitation from my grandparents. I then checked my text messages, seeing a new message from my mother, reminding me that Grandma had passed away exactly eight years before. My throat fell into my stomach and my heart began to feel heavy. Grandma June Herget was my best friend. At that time of my life, I had spent most of my weekends with her.

That morning, in the middle of my sudden shock, the angelic guidance became clear. For the first time since Grandma had died, I needed to visit the place where she had lived. About an hour later, I found myself walking through the door. As I did so, the eight-year-old memory of Grandma being taken to the ambulance on a stretcher, now at the end of her life, flashed through my body.

Now, on this day, I walked in with Grandma's favorite flowers—African Violets in a pot—in order to show my appreciation and thanks for all this place had done for her. The Assisted Living Receptionist immediately greeted me with kindness. As soon as I tried to speak, I started crying. My armpits filled with sweat. Underneath, my breasts and my forehead had become hot and clammy. I had so many built-up tears, tears that I had not been aware of, that were still cooped up inside me from that day eight years ago. I ended up having a lovely, healing conversation with the Executive Director. As I walked out of the building, I realized how mysterious grief is and how it can feel like it comes from nowhere.

As I contemplated that week, I have given myself compassionate space to process this pool of sadness and have recognized a breakthrough. I have discovered that in the depth of this pool lives a new, more spacious consciousness—medicine for my life. Not only did my Grandma die that day eight years ago, but also the safe space I felt I was always given by Grandma to remain small. What also died that day was not really living my life to the fullest.

I had not fully processed this until that week. I was also grieving the death of a part of a "small me" that controlled my life then. There was a way my Grandma never made me wrong about any of the mistakes I made; she always accepted the mediocre life I had chosen in order to stay small. At that time, that was the love I needed.

If I am really honest, I always felt there was so much more my Grandma could convey through her eyes that she would never express while she was alive; in some ways, this supported the partial life I was living. I take full responsibility for this, and I know my Grandma is thrilled to see the courageous life I am now living. My life is now in alignment with my soul.

After Grandma's passing, my whole life changed. I felt that her truthful eyes were absorbed in my heart and soul. She instantly transformed into my guardian angel who had a lot to say, and often. She no longer let me live small. Her spirit helped me see my wings, and where I was blinded by my safe, smaller patterns and not living up to my potential. I began to understand how I was a beautiful, free butterfly with magnificent potential trapped in a cocoon. Grandma never said this in words when she was alive. Once she passed away, I began to communicate and receive love in a more conscious, woken-up way that my soul needed to hear. Grandma became a catalyst for my awakening, motivating me to make big changes. For the last eight years, Grandma has been guiding me and helping me make that transition into a butterfly. A few months after she passed away, I quit a job that had never lit me up and moved to the jungle of Hawaii, where I found my wild spirit reborn again. I learned how to meditate and found from the inside what I wanted to do with my life.

She became my "kick in the butt" to really live my dreams every day. Back to Tuesday and my amazing moment of learning. The depth of love and sadness that came up for me was a wake-up call for a huge space inside myself that was waiting to be loved and appreciated—the child in me. Over these past eight years without Grandma, I had left the child in me only partially loved and partially appreciated. That little girl had been holding onto the safety

I only felt with my Grandma. I have recognized a space and a growth happening inside me where that magical little girl knows I am more consciously here for her, loving and supporting her as Grandma did for me.

This week, I have created a Garden of Joy for her to cultivate her magic and freedom. I am pausing more and more for that wise little girl in me and offering a bigger space for her to feel, to grow, and to deal with her fears. This has been a huge breakthrough in how I relate to the complexity of grief and how I can be more and more a space of love for those parts of me that are longing for love. I can now tenderly offer that as guidance to myself, my Garden Of Joy clients, and to the world from a deeper, more optimal healing space.

Grandma June Herget, I feel you with me every day and appreciate how you continue to help me find my wings and expand my flight. I loved you and will always love you with all of me! That is my most beautiful life lesson. I am lighting a candle and honoring tonight.

About Sommer Joy Ramer

Sommer Joy Ramer is the Founder Of Garden Of Joy and Co-Founder of SINE, Synergized Impact Network Exchange Alliance and Compassion Games International. She is committed to holding a space for quantum healing, guiding individuals to the Garden Of Joy all over the world.

What are you doing now that makes Peace On Earth by 2030 possible?

She has a Bachelors Degree from Western Washington University in Therapeutic Recreation, which continues to takes our projects and campaigns to new heights, guiding individuals, teams, communities, and organizations to achieve their ultimate dreams while illuminating optimal wellbeing and serving a better world.

Sommer has achieved self-mastery in Nia Technique as a Nia Black Belt Teacher, where she continues to support individuals and communities to align with their highest calling and embodied compassionate being. She brings Nia into ecstatic, healing, authentic community experiences through the medium of Dance Arts, Healing Arts, and Martial Arts. Sommer Joy Ramer dedicates her multi-dimensional life, actions, and energy to optimal beauty for future generations of all sentient beings.

Website: Compassiongames.org/who-we-are/
Facebook: StepIntoYourGardenofJoyCommunity

21

The Enlightened Women Enlightened You Summit Unpacked

Contributed by Dr. Ruth Anderson

The following is the transcript from an Angel Heart Radio broadcast of October 17, 2019 called *Bringing A Divinely Guided Summit to Fruition*—with Deb Goldberg, Teri Angel, and Dr. Ruth Anderson.

Deb: Welcome, everyone to Angel Heart Radio. I'm your host, Deb Goldberg. And it brings me great pleasure to be here with you today.

And it's an honor to serve you in the highest way that I can by bringing you the messages of Divine Love, blessings for your life. You are dearly loved, cherished, and blessed.

We are having an awesome show tonight about the summit that we have all been involved in. Teri and Ruth and I. It was so magical. It was called Enlightened Women ~ Enlightened You Summit. And can you imagine being divinely guided by Archangel Michael, to create a summit and have him direct all of the timing and your steps to bring it to fruition? And this is exactly what Dr. Ruth Anderson experienced in creating this summit.

So, tonight, we have a special guest, Dr. Ruth Anderson, who is the founder of Enlightened World Network and is an international best-selling, award-winning author. And we have Teri Angel, Happiness Coach, energy healer, medium, author, and motivational speaker. It's so awesome to be here with you guys again. There has been so much in the past month of September and leading up to that and the closing of the summit that was just an amazing experience and actually a privilege for me to be part of.

And I thought it was important to have a show so that other people could understand what it's like to be guided by Divine Presence. And what it's like to actually be asked to do something that you've never done before, that there's a learning curve of all the pieces that needed to come together to put a summit together because I'm sure other people that are listening in would like to do a summit or retreat or something like that.

There are so many moving pieces to it that it can feel overwhelming. So I thought this would be just an awesome show to really understand the whole experience and what you got from it. And with Teri and I being part of this experience, what it meant to us, and that it's just pure joy. It was pure joy.

So I think what we can start with is, is that we each talked about having an intention for this day. We set our intentions every day for the summit. And then each one of us had an intention for today. So Ruth, did you want to start with the intention?

Ruth: Sure. First, I just want to say I could not be happier than to be sitting here looking at my two beautiful soul sisters, and knowing that there are others (I am getting goosebumps even saying that), but knowing that there are other people listening to this that we hold dearly, and that Archangel Michael and Divine Mother hold dearly. So I am absolutely thrilled to be here with you. As we were talking about an intention for this time, what I heard was... well, first, Teri was saying that we're all one, and we truly are all one and we're all connected to each other through Spirit, through love. And what I heard then is that yes, we are all one, but our relationships with the spiritual divinity are all a little bit different. So I can't look at Deb and be competitive or wish, "Gosh, I wish my relationship with Christ was like hers is," because my relationship with him is different than hers is, or my relationship with Archangel Michael is different than Teri's is or Divine Mother. And they're all just different. So one thing is not to compare what our soul sisters or soul brothers have in relation to the spiritual divinity, but to really stand in the knowingness of our own relationship with the spiritual divinity. And then the other thing that they told me was that even for me, I know the relationship I have with Archangel Michael, Divine Mother, Christ, God, the other archangels, and even my communication patterns change with them on a daily basis. So just because it happens to be the way it is one day or one month or one year, don't think it'll always be that exact way. Just be open to change, be open to staying current in your conversations with them. So I guess that's my intention.

Deb: And it's really important because we also learn not to compare with each other and that we're all going to have the unique experience of Divine Presence. And there's no wrong or right, and each one of us has our own individual curriculum that we're following. And so we're going to be led, and we're going to integrate with spirit in different ways. So yeah, great point. Thank you. And Teri, would you like to share?

Teri: Absolutely. Hello, everyone. Oh my goodness. I have so missed setting an intention every day. We did this every day during the summit. And it was so awesome and so wonderful. So as I was tuning in and just listening to what this is all about tonight, what we want to get out as a message tonight, I heard the intention of being connected, just like Ruth said. Yes, we are living in an individual human body, but our spirits are so connected on that soul level, that once we do make that soul connection here on Earth, we feel that. So that is what I would like to set. The intention is for everyone that hears our words tonight to really feel that connection on a soul level. You know, we may look different, we may sound different, but really we are all part of Source, of God. And just keeping that foremost in our minds, then that brings that connection to us in such a way that you know, the human brain can't comprehend it, but our soul knows. And if you've ever met someone and you just know them, you just have no doubt. That's how it was for me with Deb and Ruth. And that's how I think a lot of our participants felt when they were hearing our words and hearing the messages. They just knew us. And I love that because that is our souls connecting. So that is my intention for the summary of the summit as well as for this broadcast. Let's all just connect and feel into that beautiful soul energy and just share love together tonight... and be immersed in God's love.

Deb: It's so beautiful. Thank you, Teri. I so agree. I think there was such a feeling of oneness throughout the summit too, like with all the speakers. As I was watching each one I was falling in love with each speaker that was talking, and I was like, "Oh my gosh," and with some of them there was so much similarity in our stories, and it was just pure love. So you could feel the oneness and what a great feeling because we don't get to feel that all the time. So when you do feel it, it just feels so good... knowing that you are soul to soul, spirit to spirit. You are in this oneness of love that is so joyful. And I just love the connectedness that I have felt with you both and everyone.

So the other part of the intention is: Jesus said that it was really important to really take in the presence that is inside of each one of you; that every single person has the ability to connect to the divine presence. And the love and guidance that is there for each person are so beautiful and so amazing. And it actually could feel overwhelming at times because we're not used to that level of love on a human life. So it is just really wanting everybody to understand that you too can have this divine guidance and divine love 24/7. It never leaves. It's always there. And it can enrich your life in so many ways; heal you of things that you feel like you need to be healed from and just expand yourself into so much more joy and love that you don't know what is possible. It's so enriching. So that is the intention that I received today. And they all go together so beautifully, don't they?

Teri: They really do. It's almost like I'm seeing this thread going from each of us from heart to heart, it's all just tied together. And that's how our intentions were: they all tied together.

Deb: Yep, they were. And I can feel it and that's what I think other people felt in this summit. I think what's really amazing about what was created in this summit is your making it about real women living real lives connected to spirit, walking with spirit, and that is what we're talking about here too. It's that our lives can be a roller coaster sometimes. And sometimes it's not. And it's wonderful. But it's about having that guidance and love all the time knowing that it's there that you can always turn to it.

And so I think that's what was really, really important about this summit, Ruth, is that it was about everybody being real, being themselves.

Ruth: Right. Is it OK if I just jump in here? Just this morning, I was remembering back to April. So here we are in October, and back in April, I was getting hints. I was getting little messages of something that was coming down the pike. And I heard, *"Why don't you go get a new haircut?"*

I thought, "What? Since when? Since when, Archangel Michael, do you care what my hair looks like? OK, you think I need a new haircut? I'll go get a new haircut." So I did.

And then I went shopping at the mall, and I was in a clothing store. And I was looking at a shirt, and I heard, *"Look at that coat."* And I looked at the coat, and it was a beautiful coat. It was a blue brocade and nothing that I would ever buy; it was just beautiful.

And I said, "Yes, that's really pretty."

And Archangel Michael says, *"Go try on the coat."*

I said, "I'm not going to try on the coat because I am not going to buy the coat, so why would I try it on?"

Again I heard, *"Try on the coat."*

OK, so I tried on the coat and of course, it fit, and it was beautiful.

I said, "OK, well, yeah, this is nice, but I'm not going to buy it."

And Archangel Michael says, *"No, buy the coat."*

I said, "So, where would I wear this coat to? I just don't dress up like this. Where would I wear this coat to?"

And he said, *"Buy the coat."*

I said, "Well, OK, if I buy this coat, will you give me something to wear it to that has to do with my work with you?"

And he answered, *"Yes."*

OK, so I bought the coat... more than I have ever spent on one piece of clothing... but that's OK, Archangel Michael's telling me to do this.

So then, over the next couple of days, I heard, *"You're going to start interviewing a bunch of women."*

Well, I had interviewed over 100 men and women before, but this was just women. This is different. So, "OK, why am I interviewing just women?"

I heard, *"Real women... living real lives... walking with spirit."*

And I thought, OK, well, that's a great tagline. But what does it have to do with anything?

And then I heard, *"You're going to do 31 interviews."*

OK, and this was rolling out day by day in meditation. I'm taking notes through all of this. And I said, "Well, who am I interviewing?" And I literally started hearing the names of women that I knew. Some of them were just acquaintances. I didn't really know them, but acquaintances, and I wrote them all down. But there were only 25 names. And I thought, OK, well, how am I supposed to get 31 interviews out of 25 names? How was that supposed to work?

I heard, *"Well, just go get started."*

So I started connecting in with these 25 women and I said the strangest invitation. "Archangel Michael wants me to interview you for this series."

I had gotten the name Enlightened Women ~ Enlightened You Summit. I said, "I don't know what we're talking about, but I'm supposed to interview you. Are you open to that?"

And every single one of the women said things like, "Yep, getting goosebumps," "Yep. This is so in alignment," "Yep. I was talking to Archangel Michael this morning."

So that was easy. The first 25 were very easy. And then when I got to Karen Palmer, I don't even know how I got to Karen Palmer, because I didn't know her before, but somebody had set me up with Karen Palmer. So then Karen says, "Well, I know some other women that might be perfect for the show."

And I said, "Well, give me the names. I'll take them to Archangel Michael. We'll see what he says."

So I took those six names to Archangel Michael and it was, *"Yes, yes, yes, yes."*

Then I heard, *"Do all of the interviews in July."*

I thought, 31 interviews in July... not a problem.

"Oh, and they all have to be video."

"Video? I don't do video."

"Do only videos from now on."

And then I thought, "Oh, that's why the haircut. Right, because now I'm going to be on video."

So, I connected back with these women, and I said, "OK, we need to do this in July," and I literally just started scheduling them in on days in July.

And then the morning of each interview, I would sit in meditation and say, "OK, Archangel Michael. I'm interviewing Pamela Olivia Brown today. What am I asking her?" I didn't even know Pamela, really, other than just her name. "So, what are we talking about?" And I would hear what we were supposed to talk about. And it wasn't until probably three weeks into the 31 days of everyday interviewing that I realized that there was a curriculum that was being followed. And it was fascinating (I got goosebumps saying that). It was fascinating. Seeing how one woman, where they left off, the next interview would start, and it just built this amazing curriculum. And I fell in love with every single one of the women.

Every day in meditation, I would hear something else. So a couple of weeks before it was supposed to start, I heard, *"So now we're going to build a community between the speakers."*

And I said, "Well, how are we supposed to build a community between the speakers?"

And I heard, *"Have a Summit Summit."*

I said, "That's great. What's a Summit Summit?"

And Archangel Michael said, *"On Zoom, bring all of the speakers and invite them in two possible times that they can just come in and look at each other and hear each other's stories."*

OK, fine. So we invited all of the speakers to two different Summit Summits, and between the two times almost every single person showed up, and they started to get a feel for each other.

And at the same time, Archangel Michael would say things like, *"Tell Linda Dierks to meet Teri Angel."*

I thought, OK, so I would Facebook message and say, "Hey, Linda, you're supposed to get to know Teri," and I just left it to those people to do that if it felt like a fit to them.

Then I started hearing, *"OK, now we're going to build community between the people who are the members who are going to be watching this."*

I said, "How are we doing that?"

And he said, *"Facebook, you're going to create a Facebook community for the members."*

And then I would hear things like, *"And we'll wait."*

"OK, you want me to do that right this second?"

And I heard, *"Yeah, we'll wait."*

So I would send off messages to different people who could help me build it. And then they would say things like, *"Well, now write a Facebook post."*

I said, "OK, what's it saying?"

And they literally would just channel to me whatever I was supposed to be saying. So that's really how the month leading up to the summit happened. And then, so we were going to start the summit September 1, so about the middle of August, they said, *"OK, now for the next 10 days you're doing a Facebook Live with one of the speakers, inviting people to come to get an idea of what this might look like."*

I responded, "OK, fine."

So I sent it out to the speakers. I said, "Hey guys, I'm looking for 10 people to do Facebook Lives with me." And people signed up for the days.

And then Archangel Michael said, *"OK, so now the days of the summit where you're playing somebody's video, so like September 1, which is Deb Goldberg, have Deb do a Facebook Live with you on that day and watch the video together and then have a Question & Answer time."*

And I thought, OK, that's a great idea... and we might have about five or six speakers willing to do that. We had everybody but two speakers sign up. So we ended up with, I think, 50 straight days of Facebook Live. None of which were my idea. And it was truly magical.

So that was really how the summit rolled out. And I can tell you every single email that got written, every single Facebook post, every single Facebook Live... what we were supposed to talk about... the questions that were being asked... every single bit of it was downloaded from Archangel Michael. I have never experienced: A) such micromanaging, because it was truly micromanaged, and B) such brilliant knowledge of timing.

Had Archangel Michael told me in April that I would be creating this summit and all of the myriad of duties and details that went into creating it, I would have said, "I don't want to take that much on." I had no idea how time-consuming it would be. And I never could have figured out the timing with which it would all come together. It was brilliant in the mastermind.

Deb: Wow. Wow. That is so fascinating. And I understand that to some degree, just because of being, having books dictated to me, not having to do a whole summit and learn how to use technology and all the other things that went along with this. So along these lines, the steps, all these steps that you're talking about, how is that affecting you?

Ruth: I felt like I was writing a second doctoral dissertation because of the hours that it was taking. And it was summer, which was kind of good and kind of not good because my girls were off school. So there were times that they would want my attention. But I had to edit a video or I had to write up this thing. So I felt in some ways, like, that wasn't how I might have wanted to spend my time. But what I can tell you because I was not as readily available, both of my daughters' relationship with their father, my husband, got much stronger. So that was really a bonus or benefit that frankly wouldn't have happened if I had been available every time they would have wanted.

Deb: Right. You just never know what the other outcome is that is happening from what you're experiencing.

And you can look at it as well, "I don't know that this is a great thing." But something wonderful that you would not have thought of comes out of it. Right?

Ruth: The other thing for me, Deb, was I had no idea how intimately involved the spiritual divinity is willing to be... no idea. And there were a couple of times that I was literally up against a deadline of... I don't even remember what it was... something I had to write for somebody or something. And I'm looking at like 10 minutes before I have to get this in. Oh, it was editing one of the videos. It was the hardest video to edit. And I finally just went, "OK, I give up. You tell me. Am I keeping this part in? Yes or no? Am I keeping this part in? Yes or no? Is there anything I'm taking out of this part? Yes or no." And literally, that's how we flew through that editing, because I completely had to give up control.

Deb: Hmm. And it is amazing because the Divine Presence wants to have all of the control. That's part of what this is. So many times we struggle to do something, we can't let go of control when you have it right there to tell you what it is that you could do and make it easier on yourself. But we don't allow ourselves to do that all the time. Because we get into what we're doing or we like what we're doing. And then we forget, oh, there might be a better way, or I'm making this harder than it needs to be.

It is intimate from the thing that you think is the most minute, silly thing. What to eat that day... how to make something... it could be things that just don't make sense that you would talk to God about or the Divine Presence that you're talking with. And it wants to be involved in everything that you do. It is so loving and so, so unbelievable to know that you are not alone and don't have to live this life managing it by yourself at all.

So, how many hours did you spend doing video editing?

Ruth: There were actually 34 speakers, but 31 videos because there were two videos that had two speakers together. Each video took at least three hours to edit. There were probably about three or four of the videos that literally took five or six hours to edit. When you take that chunk of time out of every day plus all of the other communication that was going on, plus, creating all of the emails that went out, plus the Facebook Live events, there were many days that I was working on the summit for like 18 hours a day.

And I had no idea what I was getting into. And when I interviewed Mira Rubin, God bless her, this was back in July. And she said, "Oh, man, I just finished doing a summit." She said it took so many hours.

And I thought I haven't even given any thought to how much time this is going to take. I thought we were going to start showing videos on August first. And I went, "OK, wait a minute, Archangel Michael. Can we rethink this? Can we not start showing videos until September 1? Because apparently, I have no idea what I'm in for."

And the answer was, *"Yeah, OK, that's fine."*

But had I not gotten that month's grace? I have no idea what quality product we would have been putting out there. It just wouldn't have been possible. So thank goodness Mira gave me the heads up that I had no idea what I was doing!

Deb: And I guess at some level, you didn't and you were totally guided and it all worked out in an unbelievable way.

Teri: It really did.

Deb: It is amazing. It's funny because I could see getting all caught up in the momentum of the love and the joy of doing what you're doing, and at the same time looking at like, there's so much to do. And become stressed over that, or feeling like you can't see your girls, or because I know how labor-intensive this was to do.

Ruth: Well, it was funny, I have to tell you, because I would get messages from Archangel Michael through the other speakers. And one of them was Anayah Joi Holilly. As I was interviewing her, I think it was actually during the interview or pre- conversation before, but she said she's getting this message. She's getting this download. And she says, "I can so see you really professionally packaging this summit."

And she adds, "No, no, I mean, really professionally packaging this… No. I mean, really, really professional."

I thought, OK, apparently now we are really needing to look professional. I hadn't even thought about how it was going to be coming out. So, of course, I got with my technology person. I said, "Sue, you have no idea how professionally prepared this has to look."

I just kept getting messages from different people. I thought, "OK, whatever you're saying, I'm taking it. It's all good."

Deb: And you did have some good technical support?

Ruth: Sue Seecof and Dido Clark. Mm-hmm. They are my mainstays.

Deb: They did an awful lot of work. And then on top of it, there are two anthologies.

Ruth: Right. Another piece of it. Right. I don't even remember when this information came out. It was sometime in August and I heard, *"You all are going to write a book."* First, I was told it was one book. So it would be an anthology, and whoever from the summit wanted to could write a chapter and have it in this anthology. And it was just like a day or two later I heard, *"No, you're really creating two."*
"OK, fine."
So we're in the midst of that right now, pulling together the chapters for the two anthologies, and the series is called *Gateway to an Enlightened World*. One of them is *Collective Life Lessons to Support Planetary Transformation*, and one of them is *Collective Life Lessons on Personal Transformation*. So they've got a bit of a different feel about the two of them. I was told what to use for the covers. So you know, obviously I had a lot of support from Archangel Michael and two particular Earth Angels, Andy and Rudy, they were sort of my graphics team. And so the covers are going to look really nice. And the plan is that they will be launched in November and for

sale for Christmas gifts. So that part of the summit is still happening.

One of the really amazing pieces of the summit came together as I would be down here (in my office) interviewing somebody for Facebook Lives. I would close my eyes and envision who was here with me. Archangel Michael was always here. Divine Mother was always here. Other times other people's spirit guides would show up. We had animals, pets that had passed on who had been owned and loved by the speakers or the summit participants. They showed up, which was really cool.

And Divine Mother introduced us to a healing pool which was absolutely divine. It looked like it was surrounded by a red rock quarry almost. And it was a natural pool. Although, you know in the ethereal realm, my saying, "Natural... " What does that mean? I don't really know, but it's funny to say it didn't feel man-made, but it didn't.

And she would be there during every Facebook Live event we did. And spirits... souls would come to her and receive healing. And it was the most beautiful thing, and I could close my eyes when the video was playing, I would close my eyes to get a feel for who was showing up at the healing pool. And it was always connected to the video that we were watching.

I remember the day of 9/11. We did a quiet intention for that, and I saw spirits showing up. Some had suitcases and some had briefcases. I have goosebumps even saying it. People that were on the plane that crashed was part of 9/11... people working in the buildings working on 9/11 showed up in spirit to receive healing. And every day more and more would come to this healing pool. And it just felt like my office space just kept expanding and expanding with spirit and divine love. It was absolutely beautiful.

So a couple of days before the end of the summit, Neelam Minocha was our guest, and as we were watching her video, I closed my eyes to see what was happening at the healing pool. I literally saw the roof, as if it had a roof, lifted off. And all the souls there at the healing pool just rose and basically moved on to another level of awareness and expansion. And it was stunning. And I knew that that had to do with the magnificent power that Neelam has in the work that she's doing.

And then the last night, the closing ceremony was absolutely outstanding. I wore my blue brocade coat as Archangel Michael told me to. Deb, Teri, Archangel Michael, Divine Mother, and I worked together to plan the ceremony. As the speakers and members came together around their computers, we all came together in spirit around the healing pool. In spirit, we were all dressed in white robes or gowns, almost like Goddesses. Each person had an angel and a spirit guide with them. There were healing taking place and people just totally submerging themselves in the healing powers. It was lovely. We had elementals that I hadn't ever seen before… even their royalty showed up. We had dancing… I saw "reeds of light" dancing on the healing waters. It was an absolutely sublime evening.

And when I woke up the next morning and checked in at the healing pool, I saw many beleaguered dancers, in spirit with angels and spirit guides altogether. It was the biggest love-fest. It was fabulous. So yes, what an honor to be sitting and being able to watch it come together. And to know that, in some way, I was involved in making it happen. And each of the speakers had a part, and each of the participants too, in making it happen. It was a really profound experience for me.

Deb: It is beautiful. And the way you describe it is what it was. It is the way we experienced it too. And what I thought was really interesting is the way that I saw it, is one of the books that you wrote with Open Clinic. And this summit seemed to be, with the healing pool and people getting healed in the ethereal spirit. And then, you know, here it is. That this is your vision that you've been given in the ethereal and then it actually became real here through the summit. The whole vision just unfolded into your life, and to all of our lives. It was just exquisite to really think about that... to have a vision that you've been given, and watch it unfold in front of you.

Ruth: Right, my book was called *One Love: Divine Healing at Open Clinic*. And it was about a place in the ethereal realm where the archangels and Divine Mother would be there and receive souls that came in for healing, and those souls came from Earth as well as from the Cathedral of Souls where those who have passed on are living in spirit. It is so fascinating for me to experience it on the one hand and then to experience it here in the round with people in bodies, like yourself, that are also experiencing it. So, so cool. So cool. It was powerful.

Teri, you were an integral part of this too. You were part of probably almost every day with the speakers and helping out on Facebook Live and setting intentions. Tell me about your experiences of being involved in the summit.

Teri: Yes, I was trying to think how that even happened.

Ruth: I'll tell you exactly how that happened. When Archangel Michael said, *"Do Facebook Lives for 10 days before the summit starts,"* I had never done Facebook Live. I was thinking, who can I have with me to do this? And so I had asked Karen Palmer and Sheri Myers. And then you did one of the days of Facebook Live with me. And I had been trying so hard to figure out how to make Facebook Live successful because I hadn't figured that out. I knew I could pre-record it, but then it wasn't really live. So getting finally with Ivana Vozzo Morano, she was a trooper. We spent seven hours together trying to make Facebook Live, live.

And then when I finally was able to figure it out, I think it was the day that I was talking with you on Facebook Live before the summit started. And you knew so much about it. I realized this woman knows about it. If I could just harness her and have her work with me on these, then I could breathe easier for each of the days that the summit happens. And Archangel Michael said, *"Teri and Deb, bring them in and increase their ministry."*

And so I reached out and asked you, Teri, "Would you consider please being with me on each of the Facebook Live Events? Because I don't know what I'm doing." And then through talking with you and you setting the first intention, it was like, absolutely, we need to have an intention set for every single show.

And the intentions were an important part of each show. Then there were a couple of days here and there that Deb filled in. And then it became, Oh man, this threesome, this is a thing. And so we would work together on the intention setting and then created with the divinity, the closing ceremony. And there was such power in bringing the three of us together with the spiritual divinity. It was like a force to be reckoned with.

Teri: Yeah, it really was. And, you know, I didn't know when we did that first intention that it was going to be an everyday thing. And it really it just took on a life of its own. It's like as soon as I knew that, you would tell me who the speaker was going to be the next day and, you know, I didn't really know a lot of these ladies, I knew a few but not a lot. I would just ask God, "OK, what does this intention need to be about? What does it need to say?" And the words just flowed. I didn't have to think about it. I didn't have to try to make something up. I just sat there with a pen and paper, and it just came out. So then I would send it to you or I would send it to the two of you. And we would all just find that perfect wording.

I think the intentions really touched people every day. And I've missed doing that. I was telling Deb this earlier, I really missed every day, just sitting and listening to that voice that just said, *"This is what it needs to say... "* and writing it all out. But this has been such a profound experience. And when you first contacted me, you know and said, you want to interview me, I'm going, "OK, good." You know, we're going to do an interview. I had no idea what I was in for. But it really has been life-changing. It really has been just such a beautiful experience and very professional. Very. And I love the cards. We didn't mention the cards.

Deb: Or the journal.

Ruth: I've got them right here. One of the things that I heard was to create cards and a journal... have the speakers all be included. I had no idea how to make cards or journals.

Then I was given the gift of Sue Broome, and Sue Broome makes cards and journals. So she helped to make these and what I love about these cards, for one, there's a beautiful blessing, which was given by Archangel Michael, for anybody reading the cards. Each of the speakers has a card with a quote, their favorite story, their favorite saying. And then also there are angel cards. There are six angel cards with channeled pieces that I was given to share. So they really mean a lot. These cards are just so heartfelt.

Deb: Why don't you read the blessing for us?

Ruth: This particular blessing was given to everybody now at this point, and everybody who was involved with the summit, everybody who was at the closing, and now here on Angel Heart Radio. This blessing came from Archangel Michael.

May it be with the blessings of God, the universe, Divine Mother, Archangel Michael, Archangel Gabrielle, and Archangel Raphael, that you, beloved of God are anointed with love, light, and blessings, to step further into your role of sacred being. This blessing is bestowed upon you such that you and all souls will be transformed through love and light. May every action taken and every word be said for the highest good of your growth, divine purpose, and for all involved. May you always seek guidance and counsel when you are unsure of your way in love and light, Amen.

Teri: I have to tell you, I had purchased some extra card sets to give as gifts. And I gave one to a very dear friend of mine, somebody that helped me a lot through my cancer journey. And she sat there; she opened the package, and she spread them out. And the card that she picked out was from Archangel Michael. She just started crying because he's so involved in her life and guiding her, and it was just perfect. I mean, she just said it made her day.

So I know these cards have power. If anybody out there that's listening has not ordered a set yet, please order them because they are wonderful and the message is in there. I love it. I read one every day just to get into the energy on it.

Ruth: And this is the *Enlightened Women ~ Enlightened You Journal*. And similarly, each page has, well almost every page, has a quote by one of the speakers or an Angel channeling and then there is a beautiful sign on the back that was channeled to me by Divine Mother. It says: *"Don't do... just be." "Don't think... just listen." "Don't seek... just love."* I love that.

Deb: We probably should let people know that they can order those cards, and the journal if they're interested, and it will be great for Christmas gifts or Hanukkah or anything that's coming up over the next couple of months for the holidays of people looking for gifts. It's not just for adults. You can use them for your children, your grandchildren, your friends, or relatives that might really appreciate having a daily card to look at an intention.

Ruth: Thank you. So the way to do that is go to www.enlightenedworld.online and you can order the cards and the journals as well.

Deb: Maybe we could touch on a little bit about the closing ceremony. And what I found fascinating that I shared with Ruth is that it fell on the last day of Rosh Hashanah, which starts for the Jewish people. It starts with the atonement and Yom Kippur, and it is all about atoning and forgiving yourself for your sins, if you believe in that, during the year. And then it's about getting your name into the Book of Life.

And I said you're not going to believe this but the ceremony that we did, part of it was getting your name into the Book of Life, and Ruth read all of these names, and I said, "Do you believe that it is happening on Rosh Hashanah and getting ready for the holiday for that?" The synchronicity was pretty amazing.

Ruth: The ceremony was downloaded to me by Archangel Michael a couple of years ago. And when we put together the summit closing, I was told to do the Ceremony of Light. Part of that is having everyone in spirit in a circle. And behind them were the archangels and spirit guides, and what were called Angel Runners. And as I said each person's name, that Angel Runner behind them would take off and go up to wherever I couldn't see. And they would carry that person's name up and then it was recorded into the Book of Life. And I was told that by having your name in the Book of Life, what that meant is that when you go into prayer or meditation, that the spiritual divinity says, *"Yes, I know you."* And there is that instantaneous, *"You belong. We love you. You're part of us."*

And so that's how it was presented to me. And honestly, I had not even heard of the Book of Life in any other context until Deb told me this after the ceremony. So, that was really cool.

Deb: What was so amazing too is that Teri and I channeled all of the healings, the clearings, the chakra clearings, which was amazing because I've never done that before. And everything just seemed to gel, because part of that ceremony was celebrating you and all the beautiful work that you did and bringing your vision to fruition. And that you carried it off with such honor. I felt like you made every speaker feel so important and honored. And that you know it was just such a gift to be in the presence of all of this happening and such leadership that you had given through this. So, really, the ceremony was a tribute to you for what you've done in creating this.

Also, what was really interesting is that you started to get sick or you had this cough for a while towards the last end of the Facebook Lives.

Ruth: Right. I didn't think it was a typical cold, as the symptoms would worsen when we were doing the Facebook Lives. Archangel Michael told me that I was physically carrying the ascension symptoms of that which folks in the summit had released. I was told, during the closing ceremonies, to clear those even further from the folks that were there and through me too, frankly. So that was a beautiful piece of the ceremony, the clearings of all of those symptoms that folks had held on to... the anger, and the shame and the guilt, the hurt feelings, and feeling abandoned, and feeling unloved. And it was very powerful.

Deb: There was such a healing component from the summit throughout it, of each speaker being able, I know even for myself speaking, because I would get fearful about, "OK, I'm going to have an interview, and it's going to be videoed and, you know, how am I doing?" And because, you know, I'll have confidence issues come up at times as we all do, and to sit and watch our videos was pretty amazing. I know, just from a speaker standpoint of actually seeing myself, and saying, "Wow, this turned out a lot better than I ever thought it would." And watching other people talking about their stories and what they've been through in their healings. It just created even more healing for the speakers, not just the participants. It was such a release and then you had Keleena Malnar do this amazing Light Language that I felt lifted some more healing and Neelam... There was just so much for all of us. It wasn't that we were just the speaker.

Ruth: Right. Right. The speakers were all handpicked by Archangel Michael. And I believe it was not only for what they could bring to the table but also for what they could get out of it, as well. It really seemed to be as important as what they were getting out of this opportunity. So I would say too, if anybody is interested in being able to watch the summit that has not yet participated in that, you could check that out by going to www.enlightenedworld.online so you can purchase the summit to watch all of the videos.

Teri: I love what you just said, Ruth, because that's the way energy healing works. If you're the person, the conduit for the healing to take place, you get just as much healing as the person that's in front of you, that you're working with. So I understand and know now that's how the whole summit was. And thank you, Deb, for bringing that out to light because it really was all about healing. No matter what the topic, what the person had been through, it all came down to healing, putting that healing energy out into the world, and then receiving it back to us as speakers. It was just a beautiful journey; the whole thing was so beautifully orchestrated. You know, we talked about how it flowed, how it started with one topic, and it was all divinely orchestrated to flow the way it was supposed to flow.

Ruth: So I think that's part of why we weren't quite ready to let it be over. There was one particular Sunday that Deb, Teri, and Sue were doing an event because our speaker couldn't be there. And it was amazing. And as I was watching it, I was so proud of all three of you, because you were so stepping into your ministries. And I heard in my head *"Sunday Summits,"* and it was like, "Oh, are we going to keep doing this?"

And I heard, *"Yes."*

Deb: It's just the launching pad. And also, you know, we're doing things together, like pairing with other speakers. Teri and I are doing something together, and then I'll be doing next week's show with Monica Augustine, who was one of the speakers, and we're going to be on Angel Heart Radio. Next week we're talking about healing from sexual abuse. So it'll be a very powerful discussion from both of us. And so, so many other things have come through this and joining people together. It's been really nice. It's been a beautiful, beautiful event to participate in.

Ruth: And I absolutely loved having you both with us.

Deb: I'm really privileged to have both of you here with me.

Teri: Thank you. I'm so grateful for God bringing us all together. It is a joy.

Deb: It is a joy, and I love you both dearly. I love you both. Thank you. So, when in doubt, never underestimate the power of prayer. You are being listened to and heard throughout the universe, and it always responds with infinite and eternal love. Remember to go inside and listen to your heart for the whispers of heaven. I love you and God bless you.

GATEWAY TO AN ENLIGHTENED WORLD

www.ingramcontent.com/pod-product-compliance
Lightning Source LLC
Chambersburg PA
CBHW060517100426
42743CB00009B/1354